RE-SHAPE RE-DEFINE RE-IMAGINE

RE-SHAPE RE-DEFINE RE-IMAGINE

IDEAS THAT WILL INSPIRE YOU TO 'RE-BOOT' PERSONALLY AND PROFESSIONALLY

PAT PERRY

PATSFITNESS, LLC
Mentor

Dedication

This book is dedicated to my dad, Henry J. Perry who passed away in 2009. If there were a Hall of Fame for dads, he would have been the first inductee. He was a great businessman and an even greater family man. Thank you Dad for everything. Your gentle spirit is sorely missed.

All my Love,

Pat

Contents

Preface

This book is a collection of published columns I wrote over the past 40 years. They are brief and intended to inspire you to think about how the stories and ideas can be applied to your personal and professional life.

What I have written and continue to write is focused on challenging the status quo. Much of what we do in business today is what we did in business decades ago. If we keep this up, the status quo is going to look like ... well ... the status quo.

It is so easy not to change and not to challenge. The safe approach seems like the smart approach especially when you have bills to pay. Yet how we manage business and strive for personal success is falling far short of where we could be in our companies and in our daily lives.

This book is designed as a reference guide. There is no need to start at the beginning of the book. My hope is that you refer to it frequently. You can turn to any chapter and find something that may inspire new thinking.

We all have the opportunity to be so much more than we are today in our personal and work lives. If you make incremental positive changes, magic will happen over time.

Chances are we will never meet, but please know that I wish you tremendous success and happiness each and every day. What is really cool is that along your journey you have the opportunity to make a difference for others, and as a result you can change the world.

Pat

I

WANTED: CRAZY IDEAS

———

Albert Einstein once stated that the definition of insanity is doing the same thing over and over again and expecting different results. Based on this definition, it seems like we have a lot of insanity going on these days: Too many workplaces are doing the same thing over and over, hoping for different results.

The opportunity to make quantum, progressive leaps in your local economy is staring you in the face. How you go about seizing these opportunities remains to be seen. Since the old solutions are just going to give us the same slow growth and predictable results, maybe it's time to start getting a little more sane and start implementing the crazy ideas that no one thinks will work. Here are a few examples:

Land Rush: If your metropolitan area has vacant and attractive land that is wasting away, what about giving it away for free to companies that are willing to build at the site and guarantee hundreds of new jobs in the area? Don't charge these companies property taxes for at least a decade. More people with good jobs would introduce significant dollars into your local economy. Vacant land with decrepit buildings is a sign of a dying region. It's time to clean up your wastelands if you want your region to get new life.

Bridge Sponsors: The rusted bridges over freeways provide frequent reminders of a deteriorating infrastructure. Rather than wait for your local or state governments to clean up these eyesores, invite companies to sponsor a bridge or two. Sponsoring organizations would commit to a five-year financial sponsorship of a bridge, where the dollars would be used to repaint the exteriors. In turn, the sponsors would have their company names painted on the bridges with their company tag line. It gives companies better exposure than billboards, and in the process beautifies our freeway bridges.

Free Parking Everywhere! Paid parking should become extinct. The concept is a dinosaur. Paid parking is nothing more than a nuisance and a firewall to visitors. Many of our cities are so sorely lacking visitors that the cities should be paying visitors to park.

Is Everyone In? Develop a multimillion-dollar year-long national ad campaign — sponsored by area employers and economic development groups — that showcases the livability of your region and its job opportunities. Throw in the free parking and free land, and I bet your region will have a rush of companies very interested in bringing their headquarters to your area.

Only Good News: Challenge the local newspapers to print only good news. The response would be a refreshing break from the status quo, and would likely provide record advertising sales. The one problem would be having enough staff at the newspapers to cover these stories, since there's way more good news than bad.

If you truly are a bad-news junkie, there are plenty of Internet resources to get your fill.

Tariffs: To encourage local companies to buy local products and services, place a significant tariff on goods and services purchased outside your region. Or if you prefer the carrot approach instead of the stick, provide substantial tax credits to companies and individuals that buy local.

Be Creative: There are hundreds of ideas out there to which traditionalists and naysayers might respond, "We can't do that." Well guess what? The old solutions to ongoing problems are not solving a darn thing. Throw in a lack of leadership, and you get rusted bridges, declining populations, fewer jobs, housing blight, rising crime and a host of other issues that keep us from taking our regions to new heights of prosperity.

Just remember, the next time someone tells you that your business idea is crazy, it's probably one that will work.

2

YOU CAN CHANGE THE WORLD

You may not think so, but you can change the world. In fact, you can change it every single day. It only takes one person to make a positive ripple effect in the workplace, in business and in the community. That ripple effect can be short or long-term and can inspire others to start a positive wave of change on their own. The results are impressive and can spur movements into action.

Though it appears that Americans are really good at being apathetic, I believe the opposite is true. Kudos to the upcoming generations who in many ways are taking the lead in making this world a better place to live and work. It's a crazy world out there. Some would say that it has never been worse. In my opinion, the bad stuff is just more highly publicized now.

One of the best opportunities to make positive change is in the place where you spend most of your waking hours — work. Here are a few thoughts on how you can make a difference, whether you are a leader or a non-management employee:

Quit Complaining: This costs absolutely nothing, but for some people it may be the hardest personal change they will ever make. Complaining about your job, company, co-workers or boss is probably the biggest waste of time and energy you can expend. Plus, complaining does not change a thing. If you do not like your status quo, figure out a positive solution and implement it. Otherwise, you hurt yourself and others, and in essence have quit mentally even though you've stayed at your job. Complaining is the lazy person's approach to thinking that somehow they are going to resolve problems by doing nothing. If you are one of these people, please consider taking a new approach — one that will actually work.

See the Good: I am blessed to be married to an exceptional individual who always sees the good in people. Her daily positive attitude is remarkable, and everyone who knows her personally and professionally will attest that after meeting her, they have a better day. She provides an excellent example for all of us. She's taught me that pre-judgment and negativity towards others can get in the way of developing productive and meaningful personal and work relationships. The fewer walls we put up, the easier it is to affect positive change.

Employees and Their Families Are First: If you are an organizational leader, consider establishing and maintaining a work environment where your employees and their families come before everything else, including your customers. Building great workplaces for top people begins with this core belief.

Ironically, your organization will deliver incredible customer service when the customer comes second behind your workers and their extended families. That's because you will tend to attract better-than-average employees who know how to deliver "wow" service to customers every day. Top performers really know how to produce great results at work while prioritizing their families. They want to work at organizations that share this value and will go out of their way to help drive quantum-leap business results. The traditional view of prioritizing work over family is a dinosaur.

Daily Impact: I encouraged each of our staff, at my former company, to focus on making a daily difference at work and in the community. It did not have to be anything big, just meaningful. Before they nodded off at night, I wanted them asking themselves if they made the world better than how they found it when they woke up that morning. Add all of those days up and over time little positive ripple effects turn into positive waves of change that do change the world.

We all have one shot at this deal called life. We can either decide to make a difference or hang back and hope someone else cleans up the mess. It starts with each and every one of us. So, are you letting the world change you or are you changing the world?

3

WHY GROW?

Back in first grade, when my teacher asked a tough question, my classmates and I would routinely bow our heads down, stare at the top of our desks and act like we were busy. Evidently, we were of the belief that if we looked busy we would not be called upon for an answer. I assume that our teacher must have really been amused when this occurred.

Fast forward 40-plus years, and now I find it rather interesting that this same ritual gets played out with some executive teams during the management retreats that I have facilitated. When critical questions about workplace core values, beliefs, strategies and game plans are asked, heads go down. During these awkward moments of silence, the only executive with their head upright is the CEO, sitting there dismayed, typically with arms crossed looking around the room for one of the company's other leaders to participate in the discussion. Meanwhile, the CEO's executive team members are all hoping that the CEO will be the one to answer the tough questions. It's reminiscent of how our first-grade class hoped that our teacher would give up on us and provide the answer to the class.

When I see this occur in management teams, it suggests that there could be serious issues related to communication, intimidation, shared beliefs or leadership. More importantly, the fact that the team does not answer is an indicator that some of the questions I am asking them have never been raised, discussed and answered with conviction and commitment.

Questions about issues like expanding a service, buying versus leasing, product development and branding are pretty straightforward and much easier to answer than strategic workplace inquiries. This is pretty scary when you consider that the workplace environment, philosophies and strategies should drive everything in the organization. Amazingly, these areas are seldom explored, dissected and pursued.

One question that is typically met with silence is "Why grow?" The answers from management teams are eye opening. If you think that the answer is a simple one, just ask this question at your next management team meeting.

Ironically, for many non-management employees, growth is a bad word. When growth is king and is the end-all, many employees just end up with more work and little pay improvements. To them, a fast rate of growth in the company doesn't do anything to enhance their job, workplace or life outside of work.

The "Why grow?" question is just one of many that can really get a great discussion going with your employees at all levels. If you do have a management or staff retreat coming up, try out a few of these questions with those in attendance:

- Are we committed to only hiring and keeping top performers? If so, how are we implementing this strategy?

- Do we have the right work environment to hire and retain top people? If so, how do we know?

- How do we define a top performer? Are we committed to becoming one of the top places to work in the area? Why or why not?

- Is HR a key part of our executive team and one of the drivers of our organization's success? If not, why not?

- What is our philosophy relative to employee compensation and why?

- Do we treat our employees like adults or like children?

- Why do we have a probationary period for new employees? What purpose does this serve?

- When is the last time any of us thoroughly reviewed our employee handbook and general workplace policies? Are they consistent with our beliefs, values and strategies?

- Do we trust all or some of our employees? Why are we retaining employees we do not trust?

- How would our non-management employees describe our executive team?

- If HR does not report directly to the CEO, why not?

- How do we define organizational success?

These are a sampling of questions that can provide terrific dialogue and also insight into your team's mindset, organizational understanding and individual beliefs. The answers and conclusions can set the foundation of your workplace game plan and will determine strategy and implementation of the strategy.

Incidentally, when I have facilitated these management discussions, I ask CEOs not to participate in the conversation. In addition, I ask that all laptops, smartphones and other distractions be left at the door. Both of these steps change the meeting dynamics and tend to surface what management teams are really thinking.

Consider taking a different approach at your next management or staff get-together. Ask some of the tough questions. If done right, you will know a lot more about your team and their beliefs, philosophies and day-to-day practices. That could be a good or a bad thing. But at least you'll know.

Most importantly, when the tough questions get asked, don't hide from the answers. My first-grade teacher would be proud of you!

4

BIGGEST JOB OF ALL

———————

Our economy was historically been based upon the fundamentals of supply and demand. This premise seems to have morphed into an economy today, based upon greed, corruption and fear. This may have always been the case, but I naively believed my economics professors in college. They made a lot of sense back in 1979.

Unfortunately, way too many people lost their jobs during the Great Recession and the Pandemic. Behind every one of these individuals is a dream, a family, co-workers, friends and a livelihood. Organizations have an opportunity to make a dent in unemployment that affects their cities and regions. It's a matter of being creative, taking a few risks and making sacrifice. In the long run we all benefit. More importantly, you can make a difference in someone's life today by helping someone get back to work. Here are a few ideas:

Buy Local! You may have heard this slogan over and over again.

That's because it works. From executive search to printing to architectural design, your local business community boasts great companies that can do the job. When you use an out-of-town firm when a local firm can do the project, you kill local jobs, plain and simple. Consider taking a few minutes right now and send out an email to your management team requesting a list of all your company's vendors and their locations. Ask your managers to make every attempt to work with local vendors. Buying local is one of the best ways you and your organization can positively affect jobs and your local economy.

The CEO $10/hour Pay Cut: That's about all it would take to employ a full-time intern at your organization. Better yet, hire two part-time interns (20 hours per week) and show them how great it is to work in your region. Internships are a fabulous way to start attracting and retaining young talent in your region in the short- and long-term.

Get Creative: This is exactly the time to think creatively about your business and its products and services. Historically, great new business opportunities emerged out of poor economic times. That next great idea could come out of your company. And, that great idea could spawn new employment. Now that is a great idea!

Ask! One of the great lessons that every company leader should have learned over the past few years is to include employees in decisions. In retrospect, many theorize that if employees were asked how to address an economic downturn, creative solutions may have surfaced that would have saved countless jobs. Now is a great time to get your team together. Ask them how they would approach job retention and creation in your company. They will appreciate the inclusion, and you will appreciate their thoughtful and constructive responses from your most important stakeholders.

It was disheartening to see so many fear-based decisions be the rule of the day during the Great Recession and the Pandemic. It does not have to be this way. Consider seeking creative and practical ways to retain and create new jobs during good and challenging times. Your region depends on it, and all our jobs are on the line unless we change our ways.

5

BELIEVE IT OR NOT

During my business career I was fortunate to have received some pretty sage advice from a number of really successful people. Most of the time the advice was spot on and I am thankful that I listened and heeded their wisdom.

One of the remarks made to me on several occasions is that you "cannot manage what you cannot measure." For most business projects and initiatives this works well and makes a whole lot of sense. On the other hand, running a successful business also takes gut instinct. On more than one occasion I relied on subjectivity and my gut when making an important decision.

Ironically, some of the business decisions you make, that cannot be measured on the profit-and-loss statement, provide the most impact to your business and your employees. Here are a few examples:

Well OK! Wellness and health education is not a fad and never has been. These programs work well for employees and the bottom line. It can be as simple as a walking program at lunch, healthy snacks at meetings, getting rid of the junk in your vending machines or offering occasional health tips. It does not need to be a full-blown program to be effective. Regardless of what you do, optional wellness programs made available to your staff are appreciated and utilized, and the results can be impressive. You might even save a life.

Training: I once had an executive tell me, "I do not believe in training our people. All we would do is spend money, get them trained and then they leave us!'" Wow, that statement blew my mind. If the executive really felt this way, then his organization had much bigger issues than staff training investments.

Providing training opportunities for your staff supports skill enhancement, career development and enables employees to make great contributions to the organization. A well-structured program also provides participants new perspectives to expand business relationships and demonstrates that the organization cares about their career success.

Who doesn't want their respective local professional sports teams to excel? In addition to good ownership, coaching and the right talent, we expect the athletes to practice their craft so that the team wins. Employees at companies are no different: if you want them to get better they need to practice, learn new skills and continue to think differently. Practice may not always make perfect, but without it, your untrained employees are not helping you as much as they could to succeed in the game of business.

Balancing Act: Much has been written about work-life balance and its importance in today's workplace. Yet, some traditional organizations still struggle with flexible work schedules, non-traditional hours and other programs designed to provide more balance for employees. Measuring employee performance relative to time at the job versus performance on the job is no longer accepted by top-performing employees. It's a tough transition for traditional leaders to move to a new approach to performance management. But in order to attract and retain top people these days, it is becoming more evident how critical it is to support and embrace work-life balance programs.

Truly great business leaders make many of their critical decisions based upon a combination of good information and their gut. In fact, when you study the leaders that changed industries, you find that it was more about their intuition combined with courage that moved mountains. If they had made their decisions based purely on the numbers, chances are we would not see the innovations we have today. Managing only by what you can measure minimizes risk, but in today's business environment it can be the beginning of an organizational death spiral.

Consider doing a gut check on your next big decision. Sometimes, you just have to believe and trust that feeling inside. Using the examples above, how can you possibly go wrong with healthy employees, who are well-trained and have the flexibility to put their loved ones first?

6

CHAMPIONSHIP SEASON

————————

In Northeast Ohio, where I am based, the big news that LeBron James would return to play basketball for the Cleveland Cavaliers, many years ago was met with screams and applause. It was the topic of conversation everywhere, even dwarfing the news of Cleveland being chosen to host the 2016 Republican National Convention. Such is the power of sports and a reflection of our priorities.

Northeast Ohio is, without a doubt, a sports-crazy region. The local fans cheer and support the teams as if we were perennial contenders for a championship crown. Win or lose, our fans always have an opinion about our teams, players, coaches and owners. Interestingly, the opinions shared about our sports teams contain some great ideas that should be heeded and implemented by businesses. For instance;

"Our team owners need to spend more money to get great players." This statement, repeated often over the years by area sports fans, is correct for both sports teams and businesses. If you want top performers, you'd better be prepared to pay them well and what the market dictates. Make no mistake that these days top performers at your business are exactly like free agents in sports. They have talent, a proven track record, job mobility, and they can command big bucks. Their job performance frees them up to have choices. Smart companies recognize this and pay accordingly and incentivize top performers to support their success.

"The coach stinks!" Fair or not, the coach is one of the first to go if the team is not performing to expectations. The coach is often under a microscope and depending on the season, is either the scapegoat or the hero. There seems to be a bit more patience in business than in sports for poor managers. Unfortunately, it often takes way too long for a corporate leader to be replaced if an organization's business is failing. Yet there are expectations by company stakeholders, employees and customers that an organization's leadership team knows what they are doing, will execute a game plan, and create an excellent workplace for top people. Maybe some of the impatience exhibited by sports fans and team owners for poorly performing coaches' needs to bleed over into the business world. Quicker turnover of failing corporate leaders would provide some organizations the ability to rebound quicker, save jobs and get the company back on a success path.

"Top free agents want to go to winning teams." No surprise on this one. Unless you have an athlete who only cares about the money (and there are a few), many of the top free agents in professional sports want to go where they see a fit with their prospective coach, players and team ownership. Regardless of their incredible salaries, I still believe that most professional athletes still have the burning desire to be competitive and win. That is actually what makes them great. The same can be said for great performers in business. They want to work at places where there is a challenge, where they can make a difference, where there is a significant population of other top performers, where outstanding corporate leadership exists, and where there is a history of solid financial performance.

"We have the best fans in the world." There are a lot of people who are truly raving fans of their respective sports teams. Raving fans are really important to businesses, too! Hopefully, you are growing a customer base of raving fans for your products or services. Your best customers are loyal, talk positively about you and are optimistic about their future business with you. In addition, your employees should be the biggest fans of the business. Regardless of their job at an organization, employees who are raving fans of your company are your best sales people.

There are plenty of analogies between professional sports and business, with the same key elements for success both in sports and in companies. Yet we tend to focus a great deal more emotion toward the success of local sports teams, owners, players and coaches than we do toward our own businesses. Can you imagine what would happen if it was the other way around?

7

DRAFT DAY

———————

Each year, professional football teams hold their annual draft for college football players. Across the land there is a fever pitch in cities that have a team. Draft parties are held, preceded by weeks if not months of speculation by experts and fans on player rankings and what players' teams will choose. The passion for football is impressive and unexplainable in cities that have mediocre teams.

Imagine if your business performed like a below average professional football team. My guess is that you might be closing up shop sooner rather than later. Yet despite consistently losing records, the fans of these football teams keep showing up, and have deep-seated emotions around their respective teams and players. Maybe that is why Draft Day is surrounded by so much excitement: The players chosen represent hope that things will get better. As a fan of a mediocre team, I hope that is true for next year.

So what if we could transfer the passion exhibited in the days leading up to the Draft, in our businesses, when new employees are recruited? Why isn't it as exciting to bring on new talent to our businesses as it is to recruit a new athlete?

Practically speaking, your employees have significantly more impact on your organization and quality of work life than a draft pick for your local professional football team. Consistently poor "draft picks" for your business can materially affect your customer service, product quality and other factors that can negatively impact your organizational success. "Wait till next year" is simply not an option for your business as it is for NFL teams and their fans.

Interestingly, this passion for football and sports in general is not only at the professional level. It starts early in youth programs, middle school, high school and at colleges and universities. The emphasis on academic excellence seems overshadowed by sports.

Make no mistake: The number of touchdowns, three-pointers and home runs that candidates for employment have accumulated in their scholastic sports career are generally irrelevant to employers seeking top talent. They seek individuals who excelled academically, participated in leadership activities, are involved in the community and have relevant work experience. Now, if candidates participated in sports at some level, it shows that the candidate was involved in team activities. Coupled with academic excellence, sports involvement reflects a well-rounded individual who was able to successfully manage their time.

If you talk to most successful business owners today, they will tell you that their biggest challenge is finding and keeping talented individuals. They are passionate about their "draft picks." They know that each and every person in their workforce is critical to the ongoing success of the business. There is no "wait till next year" in their mission statements. There is only today, competing in a global marketplace that is getting more challenging by the minute. Successful businesses can ill-afford bad hires. When it happens, the ripple effect can be devastating, especially in a small company.

Conversely, superstar employees consistently change the landscape of a business and an industry. We all want superstars in our town whether they are athletes in our professional sports teams or professionals in our companies. Yet real economic growth will occur when the passion for top talent in business matches or exceeds the excitement witnessed in the annual NFL draft.

You never know, one day we could witness police escorts and streets lined with people cheering on local high school Science Olympiad teams as they travel to the state championship. Maybe one day schools will have academic halls of fame, with scholars' pictures in the hallways. In addition to a sports section, perhaps newspapers will one day have a daily academic and professional section highlighting great achievements. Maybe there will be a national signing day for top academic achievers to announce which scholarships and schools they are selecting, and children will idolize those who achieve' academic and professional excellence and seek their autographs.

I know this may seem far-fetched. And isn't it sad that imagining prioritizing academic achievement over athletic achievement in this country seems crazy and will never happen? Scares the heck out of me.

8

LAB EXPERIMENT

———

Many years ago, my family made a decision that changed our lives forever. We bought a dog, a black Labrador retriever we named Nikki.

Even though my brothers and I enjoyed a pet beagle during our childhood, I had forgotten what impact these pets could have on a family. Over the years we came to appreciate how much we learned from her, even though dogs supposedly have a lower intellect than humans.

The fact is that Nikki, like most Labs, had characteristics that can apply to all of us at work. We were fortunate to have her many years and despite her age, she continued to teach by example. For instance:

- Nikki respected and treated people the same, regardless of their race, color, religion, national origin, veteran status or sexual orientation. She did not need a law like Title VII of the

Civil Rights Act to treat people fairly and without discrimination.

- She was loyal, a key ingredient in sustaining the employee and employer relationship.

- She stayed away from things that stunk. The business lesson is to stay away from bad deals that seem too good to be true.

- Nikki didn't bark behind our backs. If she wanted our attention Nikki would let us know right away. How much better would workplaces be if we cut out the hall talk and rumor mill?

- She played nice all the time. So should we.

- Nikki provided unconditional love, all the time. Likewise, employers that truly appreciate and care about their employees, thrive and improve the probability of attracting and retaining top people.

- She never took our family and neighborhood dog friends for granted. Likewise, people who consistently show up for work and put forth 100 percent effort should be appreciated.

- She loved security, consistency and predictability, as do employees at their workplace.

- She took plenty of rest breaks. A good lesson for all of us that taking time for ourselves is important.

- She never bit anyone. Employees need to be respectful of each other as should employers be respectful of their staff.

- In her younger years, Nikki was a hard worker, retrieving sticks and Frisbees until exhaustion. When you go to work, give it your all and make a positive difference in your organization.

- She was never shy about showing affection in public, and was a great listener. If you are a manager, don't hesitate to publicly recognize exceptional employee performance and listen more than you talk.

- She had a short but fulfilling life. In the big picture, our careers are also brief. We might as well make each day count and enjoy our work while making a living. If you love your job, know your job and believe in what you're doing, you won't be living for the weekend.

Nikki was enrolled and passed obedience class when she was a puppy. What an experience! There is nothing quite like watching 20 strangers with new dogs pretending to have some control over their pets. If I wasn't a part of the class, it would have been worth just pulling up a seat to watch. Interestingly enough, the dogs attending the class did not need the teaching; it was the dogs' owners who needed lessons. The dogs were, in fact, the real teachers.

We can learn much from dogs. Maybe they can't teach us how to build effective compensation systems, recruit better employees or increase profits, but they sure can provide lessons on how we should treat each other at work. I'm convinced that if dogs could talk they would make great corporate leaders. Consider how much better workplaces and the business world would be if we actually acted more like them.

9

ON-BOARDING PEYTON

Peyton is a purebred yellow Labrador retriever. When she was a pup, she exceeded all of our expectations: She slept through the night since day one, was quickly housebroken and responded to her name and simple commands.

Peyton not only joined our "human" family, but also slowly but surely befriended our other Labrador, six-year-old Logan. Suffice it to say, it was an interesting process watching the two of them get accustomed to each other.

Bringing a puppy on board with an older, more experienced dog got me to think about the stark similarities with some of the best practices I have seen over the years in great workplaces as they successfully orient their new employees. For instance:

Selection: Everyone who buys a puppy hopes that they select a dog that will grow up to be a well behaved, loving pet. There are a number of selection factors that breeders and veterinarians share that increases the probability that the puppy will be a healthy animal and a good pet. It goes well beyond the "cuteness factor"; recognizing that there is some science behind selection increases the probability of success for both puppies and new employees.

Planning the First Day (and Night): The first day and night with a puppy is tough on the human family and the dog. In fact, the first few weeks can be quite a challenge. But proper planning and preparing the welcome for the new arrival, over those first few days and weeks, definitely makes life better for both parties. Similarly, getting ready for a new employee and making them feel welcome provides a great start and reinforces the candidate's employment decision.

Planning the First 90 Days: I believe that the amount of energy and effort you put into the first 90 days of puppy ownership pays huge dividends for the remainder of their lives with you. I am not a dog expert, but I have observed through dog ownership that having a consistent game plan does work. Puppies seek direction and positive reinforcement on what you expect of them. New employees are no different. People want to know what to do and how to perform their jobs at work. The greater the clarity, the greater the odds that the new employee will be on the path to success with your company.

Buddy System: Having an older dog really helps a puppy understand what is expected in their new home. It is amazing to watch puppies mirror the older, more experienced dog and follow their lead. Likewise, having a buddy system at work for new employees is just another way to ensure that they get on the right track and accelerates introductions to other employees.

Recognition and Rewards: Owners of new puppies are quick to reward good behavior, which reinforces desired behavior. Can you imagine if employees were rewarded as often with the same enthusiasm that dog owners lavish on their pets?

Training: Ironically, I know executives who emphatically support and participate in training for their dogs, but hesitate to provide training support to their own employees. Perhaps if employees were not "housebroken" these executives would pay more attention to them.

A dog trainer once told me that there are no bad dogs, just bad owners. He believes that every dog is a product of his or her environment and every dog has the potential to be a well-behaved pet.

Likewise, experience has taught me that most people want to contribute at work, have meaningful jobs, be recognized for their performance and make a difference. In fact, every person either is or has the potential to be a top performer. So much has to do with the work environment, leadership at the top, and of course, the individual's willingness to excel.

There are great companies out there that understand these concepts, but unfortunately there are still some traditionally managed workplaces where the staff is challenged to meet and exceed their potential. Ironically, by adopting some of the basics of raising a puppy, the humans working at average workplaces would greatly benefit. This is one time when "going to the dogs" is a good thing.

IO

A BUSINESS LESSON LEARNED FROM GOLF

———

Whether you are a novice or an old pro at golf, you have likely encountered a few sand traps, bunkers, lakes, creeks and trees on the course. Besides the challenges inherent in actually hitting the golf ball, these obstacles often get in the way of achieving a good score. For instance, many golfers have experienced the intimidation of a 200-yard par three with a small lake and three sand traps guarding the putting green. Such intimidation can change a golf swing and for some, how they play the hole.

I have a friend who uses an old golf ball anytime there is a chance that he may hit a newer golf ball into a water hazard. On occasion, he will hit a ball short of the water intentionally, to avoid a penalty stroke. It's actually quite entertaining when he utilizes this strategy and hits too good of a shot that ends up in the water!

Whether it's my friend or other golfers, how we react to the lakes, trees and sand traps on a golf course is not too different from how we respond to the obstacles we face as we pursue career, organizational and personal success.

Some say that great golfers never see the hazards on a golf course. Their focus is on the flagstick, not the obstacles in their way. If by chance they do encounter one of these annoyances, they simply deal with the new situation and refocus their energies on the perfect shot to the green. These golfers have great confidence in themselves and their golf swing, which provides them an opportunity to attack a golf course, take some risks and remain focused on playing the game. Conversely, too many amateur golfers spend their time on a golf course trying to figure out their swing, rather than playing and enjoying each golf hole.

But it's not just great golfers who have excellent focus. Look around your workplace. Top-performing employees excel at what they do because they have goals and an unrelenting desire to achieve them. They have great focus and do not let "hazards" in the workplace affect their work. When they hit a few bumps in the road, they adjust and recalibrate their path to accomplishing what they set out to do.

Many of the other attributes professional golfers possess also correlate to success in business. These include consistency, practicing their craft, learning from mistakes, honesty, hard work, the right aptitude, perseverance and a positive attitude.

So as you continue on your path to career success and supporting your organization's success, consider adapting the positive attributes associated with good golf. It's no guarantee that you will always steer clear of business hazards, but when you do encounter them, the next shot you take will be one in which you are well-prepared.

One day, when you look back at your career and business scorecard, you will be proud that you played the game the right way.

II

BUSINESS BELIEFS THAT ARE BECOMING MYTHS

There is a saying: "May you live in interesting times." Though it is often suggested that the saying is of ancient Chinese origin, it is neither Chinese nor old. It is actually a Western saying, and depending on your perspective it can be interpreted as a blessing or a curse. Regardless of your interpretation, these days are indeed interesting times in business.

Big data, technological advancements, economic challenges, corruption, ever-increasing government legislation and generational differences in the workplace are just a few of the dynamics that are affecting every size business across all industries. As a result, many traditional business practices, ideas and programs are becoming extinct, making way for new, innovative and adaptive business models that increase the probability of success in this ever-changing environment.

Along the way, people are discovering that long-held business beliefs are evaporating quickly, while new perspectives are developing on success and work. Here are a few traditional beliefs that are radically changing:

Myth #1: Bigger Is Better: No longer is it a guarantee that big companies are great companies. Small and mid-sized businesses have experienced an epiphany, realizing that they can be more nimble, adaptive and creative than the big guys. The intimidation factor is gone and with it the playing field has been leveled.

In addition, top-performing candidates for open positions are seeking great workplaces regardless of size and not just eyeing a "name-brand" company to add to their resume. Today, top performers care a heck of a lot more about making a difference at work and having an impact on results. They want to be heard and be rewarded for individual and team performance. They want flexible work schedules and hours with minimal bureaucracy and little to no politics. Many of these characteristics describe smaller to mid-size organizations. The larger companies know this, and the smart ones are overhauling their HR practices and programs, work cultures, and leadership to develop workplaces that are more suited to top talent.

Myth #2: Title Reflects Performance: There was a day long ago when employees assumed that anyone with a senior corporate title was competent as well as a top performer. It was a time of unquestioned authority. But times have changed; today everything is questioned, and it should be. People occupying positions with management titles need to earn the title, not just be given a title and expect people to follow their lead. Title now equates to credibility, and if that is shattered top performers have little to no use for executives who do not do their jobs exceedingly well.

Myth #3: High-growth Must Mean Great Workplaces: The media loves to cover businesses with high growth rates, including those that merge or are acquired. Traditionally, job candidates also sought companies in the spotlight with high growth because it typically equated to new jobs. Yet the sizzle starts fading when high-growth companies are accompanied with high turnover rates of top employees.

Fast growth is fun to hear about, but incredibly difficult to successfully manage. Few companies do it really well, and those that do tend to be at the top of their industry because they are able to retain the high achievers that got them to the top of the "mountain." Today, experienced top achievers seek great workplaces first and high-growth characteristics second. In pursuit of great talent, organizations on the fast track are well advised to pay lots of attention to maintaining a terrific workplace culture and environment, otherwise their company may end up being a "one-hit wonder."

Myth #4: Hours Reflect Hard Work and Loyalty: Top performers dismissed this traditional view many moons ago. They recognize that hard work and loyalty equate to results, regardless of the hours it took to achieve those results. Smart corporate leadership have also bought into this fact and started focusing on what really matters to the organization and employees. Enlightened leadership no longer correlates time worked with company commitment.

The 40-hour work week, two-day weekend, and traditional eight-hour day are all being questioned, especially by up-and-coming generations. The traditional view of work hours and work schedules fit the definition of Dr. Einstein's definition of insanity — doing the same thing over and over again and expecting different results.

Myth #5: Customers Come First: This may be a wonderful marketing concept, but in reality, if companies really place customers first at all costs, they will lose really good employees along the way. When that happens, ironically customer service suffers greatly. Conversely, great workplaces for top talent who put employees and their families first, will create incredibly strong engagement between top performers and the company. That's when customer service actually skyrockets.

Myth #6: Stretch Payments: The traditional policy of companies stretching payments to vendors is a dinosaur. Once looked at as smart and slick financial management, it is quickly becoming a black eye to companies who want to collect quickly and pay out slowly. More and more organizations prefer to do business with other companies that pay on time. If your company really has to stretch payments, you may have bigger operational issues that are putting pressures on your cash flow. Please do not punish vendors with your inability to effectively run your company.

Myth #7: The Work Week is 5 Days: Workers are questioning the five-day work week and the traditional eight-hour day. And for good reason. They continue to be more focused on quality of life and not just work. Progressive companies are continually seeking new ways to offer flexible work options for employees. Organizations that put quality of life first tend to attract top people of all generations.

Myth #8: It's All About The Bottom Line: This one is a tough concept to swallow. Companies that are primarily focusing on their vision, strategy, mission, top-talent attraction and retention, quality and "wow" customer service find that extraordinary financial results are the natural by-products of a well-run business with the right people in place. Companies still believing the bottom line is the end-all find they are becoming part of an endangered species.

Myth #9: Employees Need To Be Company Loyal: The tables have turned on this one. Today, employees are expecting their organizational leadership to show employees daily that management is loyal to them. Employees, especially top performers, have recognized that the organization needs them more than they need the organization.

What has not changed is that success in business and in life results from hard work, integrity, honesty and empathy. Without these attributes, no amount of money, high growth or skyrocketing stock prices mean squat. The ability to look in the mirror and be proud of the way you conduct yourself daily is the ultimate performance review.

Today's constant change is the only thing not changing. That's why looking at business in a different light and dispelling old myths about how we work is the only option.

12

THE (NEAR) PERFECT EMPLOYEE

———————

As human beings, we are capable of contributing to the success of our respective workplaces and also making plenty of mistakes along the way. As the saying goes, no one is perfect. Though there is great truth in these words, I tend to believe that there are certain characteristics that provide a near-perfect foundation for greatness:

Attitude and Aptitude: Attitude and aptitude cannot be taught — people either have neither, one or both. I encourage you to seek to attract and retain people, for your company, that have both. When individuals do have both of these qualities, the sky is the limit. Chances are that these folks will end up driving 100 percent of your business success.

Know, Believe and Love: Closely related to aptitude and attitude, when employees know, believe and love what they are doing, they have near-perfect alignment with their job and their organization's mission.

Have Their Act Together: People in organizations that are top performers, likely have their act together at home and work. Positivity oozes from these individuals and they see fun challenges where others see obstacles.

Daily Difference: There may be nothing more impressive than individuals whose daily goal is to make the world a better place than it was when they found it. These individuals recognize that changing the world begins at home and with co-workers. Encourage your staff to assess their day before they go to bed at night. Hopefully most nights they are answering "yes" to the question of whether they made a positive difference that day.

No Green Monster: You know that you have a healthy work environment when people generally are happy for others' success. Jealousy towards co-workers should not exist in a healthy work environment.

Fit and Healthy: Aside from the obvious benefits of lower absenteeism and increased productivity at work, a focus on health has a plethora of intangible benefits that are reflected in the quality of their work, their ability to manage stress and their relationships with co-workers.

Raise Your Hand: Encourage thoughtful questions, feedback and ideas at your workplace. For employees to feel comfortable raising their hand, they need to know that they will not be penalized for taking a risk by sharing their thoughts. If you have hired and retained top talent, then it is imperative to create this environment, otherwise you will never hear the spectacular thoughts they are capable of voicing.

Consider assembling your own list of characteristics that improves the probability that you will attract and retain the right people for your company. The results of your corporate talent acquisition and management initiatives are the epicenter of your organization's success. Do it right and you win. Do it wrong and you are sunk.

If you start with an idea of the type of people who make sense for your company, then you really improve the odds of perfecting the creation of a workforce that has incredible possibilities. Even though nothing is perfect, it should not stop you from trying to get there.

13

POLITICALLY INCORRECT

The political election process is pretty amazing, but so different from how most private-sector businesses search to hire their top executives. If our forefathers intended top performers to be elected into government leadership positions, the process in place may not be achieving their objective.

From an HR vantage point, let's try to put the election process into perspective:

What a Country! If you work in the private sector imagine publicly seeking a new position while employed in your current job. Not only would you be seeking a new opportunity, but you would spend nearly 100 percent of your time campaigning for a new job while expecting 100 percent of your pay from your current employer. In contrast to how elected officials move up the government ranks, companies in the private sector actually expect their management and non-management employees to work at their current job, be remunerated accordingly and not spend time seeking another position while on the company payroll.

No Experience Necessary: Unfortunately, voters typically elect candidates for public office on characteristics such as personality, image, oratory skills, ability to debate and party affiliation. None of these have much to do with the ability of candidates to do the job. Contrast that to the typical recruiting process in business: These searches entail significant effort to locate top performers with real experience utilizing exacting requirements for job qualifications. Viable candidates must meet or exceed key criteria to be considered for open positions.

Cost-To-Hire: The dollars involved in campaign financing as compared to a private sector search is remarkable. For instance, the typical executive search fees for the U.S. president's position would be approximately $130,000 to $140,000. Yet hundreds of millions of dollars are raised and spent attempting to elect a candidate for a position that pays roughly $400,000. For most of the local, state and national political races it seems to be all about which candidates can raise the most money and not necessarily who is the best qualified.

Who Are We to Judge? Voters are entrusted to make good and informed decisions when casting votes on Election Day. Ironically, very few of us have any real knowledge of the day-to-day requirements and responsibilities for elected offices.

Think About It: When was the last time you reviewed a job description for an elected official's position and matched it up to a candidate's background and experience to see if there was a fit? We vote and hope for the best based on yard signs and smear campaigns. This is a pretty scary scenario considering the high stakes. In contrast, companies in the private sector put the odds in their favor of hiring a top performer by utilizing a streamlined and professional hiring process with full knowledge of job responsibilities and performance expectations.

You Can't Ask That! One of the hiring cornerstones of American business is compliance with Title VII of the Civil Rights Act of 1964, which prohibits an employer from discriminating in the workplace on the basis of race, color, religion, sex, or national origin, to name a few. Ironically, candidates for public office are judged and elected — or not elected — based on these characteristics with little regard to their actual qualifications. If American businesses approached recruiting this way there would surely be state and federal punitive consequences for violating Title VII by unfairly discriminating against certain candidates. Beyond the importance of non-discriminatory hiring practices, it would be just plain dumb to hire someone for any reason other than their qualifications to do the job.

You Did What? Thanks to the media, candidates for public office and their families are subject to incredibly invasive background checks. The media does make it personal, as do competing political party members. Fortunately, in the private sector, we utilize civilized and appropriate approaches for background investigations using professional firms. The information is kept confidential and is not utilized as a weapon of humiliation for employment candidates or their extended families.

What Makes Them Tick? During my adult life I have never heard of an elected official or candidate for public office being subject to a psychological assessment. It would be nice to know the state of mind of candidates prior to Election Day. In stark contrast, most organizations in the private sector routinely engage trained management psychologists to assess final candidates against previously established success profiles for open positions.

There are plenty of other comparisons one could make between public office elections and private-sector top performer and executive recruitment and selection. The private sector approach to hiring may not always be perfect, but for the most part U.S. companies utilize a non-discriminatory blend of science and sensitivity to seek out and select top talent. Much of the time it works pretty darn well.

Perhaps one day, our elected officials will open their eyes and see that the laws of the land combined with private-sector business savvy can yield the high-end results we so often hope for from our government. It would be a pipe dream to imagine the current election process being reformed. There is just too much money, power and control at stake. Yet a campaign to change this process would be worth supporting.

14

WATCH THE BIRDIE

There is a legendary story often told around Thanksgiving about a remarkable woman who not only salvaged a holiday gathering, but is also a shining example of how to think on your feet. This woman, whom we will call Mrs. Smith, prepared all day for her first holiday feast at her family's new home. Relatives and friends had been crowding into her home that Thanksgiving Day since late afternoon, enjoying each other's company and looking forward to a fabulous holiday feast.

Mrs. Smith had never cooked a holiday dinner for such a large group and was quite nervous about the results. Her mother-in-law was her greatest critic and was present for this momentous occasion. Fortunately, everything in the kitchen was going well and Mrs. Smith's confidence began to soar as she neared the dinner hour.

Mrs. Smith peered out of the kitchen one last time before calling everyone to their seats for the feast. The table was set

---

elegantly with every trimming imaginable in an idyllic holiday setting. Lights were dimmed, holiday music played softly in the background and all the relatives were actually getting along. How impressive this was all going to be, she thought: Finally, the perfect holiday!

One last check needed to be made in the kitchen. The turkey was magnificent. A huge bird, golden brown and glimmering with a buttery glaze. The supporting cast of sweet potatoes, mashed potatoes, gravy, stuffing, rolls, beans and cranberry sauce were ready to be presented to the awaiting and hungry crew.

It was time. Mrs. Smith proudly emerged from the kitchen to announce that dinner would be served. At once, the gallery of relatives and friends assembled at the table. Moods were upbeat, conversation pleasant, and anticipation for the annual parade of food began to climb. One by one the items that would complement the main attraction (the turkey) were carefully placed on the table and arranged for easy access. As if trumpets were sounding in a scene from medieval times, the group's attention focused on the grand entrance of Mrs. Smith with her prize turkey.

The door swung open and there she stood. It was a picture of triumph and glory. She had done it. Despite all the pressure of preparing the holiday feast, she was really going to pull it off. She stood motionless for a moment at the doorway leading into the dining room to enjoy the moment. "Oohs" and "ahhs" sang her praises as if in a chorus. Even her mother-in-law was impressed and joined in the spirit of the moment.

As Mrs. Smith took her first steps into the dining room, the unspeakable happened. She tripped on the area rug covering their hardwood floor and watched, as if in slow motion, while her turkey slipped off the serving platter onto the floor. She looked up and surveyed the faces of her guests as she sank to her knees. Looks of disbelief — and a smile from her mother-in-law — said it all.

In one swift motion Mrs. Smith scooped up the fallen bird, placed it back on the platter and remarked, "oh what a shame, I guess I'll have to go back to the kitchen to get the other one."

How many of us would have reacted the way Mrs. Smith did? The actions of the Mrs. Smiths of the world provide some valuable lessons that can be applied to business success:

- Thinking quickly on your feet.

- Keeping your cool in front of a tough audience.

- Not panicking and having the ability to adapt to ever-changing circumstances.

- Seeing potential disasters as opportunities to "wow" your clients.

- Understanding that while preparation increases the probability of success, it does not guarantee it.

- Realizing you never know when your actions will make you legendary.

Not unlike Mrs. Smith's response to tough and unexpected circumstances, how you manage yourself in challenging business situations can make the difference of being a "turkey" or "flying like an eagle."

15

WHAT COLOR IS YOUR EGG?

Every year, prior to Easter Sunday our family colors eggs and I attempt to make the best looking egg and also the ugliest. We have a lot of fun experimenting with colors and always seem to get more of the dye on the table, rather than on the eggs.

I think one of the reasons I enjoy this "holiday tradition" so much is that it takes me back to when I was a kid and also when times seemed simpler. Nothing much has changed over the many years of egg coloring; hard-boil the eggs, cool them off and then dip them in the assorted dyes for a minute or two. Simple, fun, and for a brief period of time, regardless of any natural talent, everyone who colors eggs becomes an artist.

When I was at my former employer, we also had fun with egg coloring via an egg coloring contest for our employees. Typically, three different types of colored eggs were produced by the staff:

The perfect egg – this is the egg that is one color, was dipped precisely the correct amount of time and had virtually no color flaws or cracks. These eggs were produced by employees who were known at work to precisely follow instructions, take few risks and had great pride in producing a great product in accordance with all the guidelines and rules.

The creative egg – this is the egg that had multiple colors and perhaps even glitter or a wax crayon applied. It certainly stood out, yet colors were applied symmetrically or with some well-thought out design. Employees who created this type of egg had a reputation at work to stretch the rules a bit, took some risks and challenged the status quo.

The bizarre egg – this egg had been dipped in just about every color, adorned with every type of glitter and perhaps dressed up with additional decorations. Employees who experimented with their eggs in this manner were known at work to throw the rules "out the window," took lots of risks and loved challenging tradition.

Regardless of how the outer shell looked, each of the eggs tasted exactly the same on the inside. The same can be said of people at work. Everyone is different on the outside, with different backgrounds and different skill sets. Yet, on the inside, most individuals who are working hard at their jobs have remarkably similar characteristics as they:

- Have a great attitude and aptitude
- Know, believe, and love what they are doing at work
- Change the world every day through their actions
- Are ethical and honest – especially when no one is looking
- Lead by example

- Are not afraid to take risks

- Don't "crack" under pressure

- Are results-oriented

These people are the "Good Eggs" in your business. Fill your "basket" of job positions with them and you will find that your company "hops" leaps and bounds over your competition!

16

BATTERIES NOT INCLUDED

———————

Despite the craziness associated with shopping, decorating, gift giving and errands, the holidays can still be a magical time of year for big and little kids. It is a season to enjoy, yet the hustle and bustle of year-end personal and business activities can get in the way of truly appreciating the holidays.

One of the pressures that many employers experience is what to provide to employees as holiday gifts. From turkeys to cash, the gifts vary greatly and the decision never seems easy. Yet regardless of the material items you may have or are providing to staff, consider some of the following gift ideas that will keep on giving for a long time:

- Ask your employees what needs improvement at your workplace. It's a great first step.

- Take a walk around your facility. Does it need a makeover? If so, use some bright colors on the walls, organize cluttered areas and ensure that your employees have a safe and productive workplace.

- Eliminate probationary period policies. They send the wrong message to new employees.

- Let employees know you appreciate them showing up for work and performing at high levels.

- Support a balance between work and family life for all your employees.

- Pay your interns.

- Purchase services based on value versus price.

- Purchase services and products locally. It's a great way to create and save jobs in your region.

- Pay employees fairly and competitively.

- Become passionate about developing a great workplace for top performers.

- Assess your employees' training and educational needs and budget accordingly.

- Incorporate wellness and health education into your health insurance program. You will save lives and money.

- Encourage employees to make their workplace better every day.

- Encourage your employees to take risks and reward them for their courage and results.

- Lead versus manage.

- Update your employee handbook and eliminate archaic language and employment policies that are no longer relevant.

- Surprise your employees once in a while with impromptu rewards and recognition.

- Recognize great performance often and publicly.

- Be honest and ethical in all your interactions with staff.

- Share financial information with your employees. They need to understand how your company ticks.

- Provide poor-performing employees with the support and tools they need to succeed.

- Avoid politics and destroy workplace bureaucracy whenever possible.

I'm sure there are others you can add to the list. There are so many possibilities to provide all sorts of surprises and "gifts" for your employees. Many don't even cost a dime!

Don't let the Grinch steal your business. You have an incredible ability to spread some workplace magic, making believers out of your employees that great things are possible at your organization. So next time the holidays roll around, spread some holiday cheer, enjoy the season and work on your own "nice list" of workplace improvements. If you incorporate a few of these ideas at your business, you increase the probability of a happy New Year.

17

WHO WAS THAT KID?

———————

One of the worst questions you can ask a child is, "when are you going to grow up?" Childhood is short-lived and really cool. So why in heaven's name do we want our kids to grow up so quickly? Most people I know would love to go back in time and be a kid again. You can certainly include me in that group.

Unfortunately, the innocence and magic that accompanies childhood erodes and disappears as the years tick by. As a parent, there is nothing we can do about it, except enjoy the time we have with our kids while they are young.

It's not just the magic that disappears. Our wonderful childhood imaginations become impeded by realism and the constant urgings of parents and teachers to grow up, conform and fit in. Creativity gets replaced with getting graded on how well you color inside the lines.

Before we know it, we're driving, graduating and working. We learn the ropes, try to act professionally, get paid, get reviewed,

———————

get promoted and sometimes get out. Our early career stages are filled with rules, guidelines and advisements of "how we do things around here." Employees may be encouraged to be risk-takers and be creative, but they're not sure what that means anymore. The system has wrung the inner kid right out of them.

Sometimes consultants are brought in to help employees become more creative. All of a sudden, employees and management teams find themselves climbing through spider webs made with ropes or climbing in the Rocky Mountains, all in the name of team-building and problem-solving. Clumsily, they do their best not to be embarrassed while they try to regain some of the coordination lost so many years ago. It was so easy when we were ten and we had no fear. What happened?

It's amusing to see all the books in the market on how to have fun at work. Do we really need an instruction manual on how to laugh, smile, get along and be creative in the workplace?

Yet, we are still kids inside — just a bit bigger and older. All that creativity and imagination is still there ready to work its magic. It's just been buried with years of being grown up. The challenge is to break the chains of adulthood and think a bit more like a child. If we allow employees to let that inner child out once in a while, organizations might be better off and more successful.

Consider breaking down some workplace barriers. Allow your staff to let the inner kid out, think more freely, innovate and take risks. Here are a few ways to help you rewind back to simpler times:

Lead by example. Loosen up, smile, laugh and show your employees that you are human. Look, you will be a "stiff" after you pass on, so why be one when you are alive?

Let them scrape their knees once in a while, allowing them

to take risks and try new ideas. And don't forget to reward employees for trying something different.

Eliminate corporate barriers that limit creativity like archaic employment policies, demeaning rules and layers of bureaucracy.

Take a trip to the local paint store and pick out some vibrant colors for your office. Better yet, ask your employees about your office décor, wall colors and carpeting. I'll bet you get some great feedback on how to create a worker-friendly and stimulating environment.

Consider incorporating a business casual dress code at least once a week if not daily. Remember, most kids hate to dress up.

Instead of reading the next best-selling business book, have your management team read *All I Really Need to Know I Learned in Kindergarten* by Robert Fulghum and then talk about it. The fundamentals covered in the book are terrific guides to running a highly effective and successful business.

Kids love to play and be challenged. Your employees are no different. Talk with your team to find out their ideas on how to enhance their jobs and your company's work environment. They will appreciate being asked, and you will get some great advice.

Kids really do say the darnedest things. Their view of the world often shakes paradigms, which is what those high-priced creativity consultants try to do with organizations every day. So take a step back and look at your workplace. Are you providing the kind of environment that brings out the inner kid in your employees? If not, it may be time to get out some crayons and sketch out your next strategic plan.

18

MOMS MAKE OUR DAY

My mom Dorothy was blessed and cursed with having three boys to raise with my dad. There were four guys in the house and no female companionship for my mom, other than our dog Lady. Poor woman! My mom is a tough woman and like most moms, she provided sage advice backed by a conventional upbringing with very strong traditional values.

My mother used many of the "momisms" that are utilized by moms worldwide. Here are some that mom used most often that were memorable and actually impacted the value system my brothers and I use in business:

- Did you wash your hands?

- Where are your brothers?

- Go to your room and think about what you did.

- Money does not grow on trees.

- What if everyone jumped into the lake? (We lived minutes from Lake Erie.) Would you do it, too?

- Close that door! Were you born in a barn?

- If you can't say something nice, don't say anything at all.

- Don't put that in your mouth; you don't know where it's been!

- Be careful what you wish for, it might come true.

- Don't eat those, they will stunt your growth.

- It doesn't matter what you accomplish, I'll always be proud of you.

- I hope that when you grow up, you have kids "just like you!"

- Because I'm your mother, that's why!

- If I've told you once, I've told you a thousand times.

- If you fall out of that tree and break your leg, don't come running to me.

- Because I said so.

- Just wait till your father gets home.

- No dessert until you clean off your plate.

- I've got eyes in the back of my head.

- Don't think I don't know what's going on.

- Just you wait until you have kids of your own; then you'll understand.

- I slave for hours over a hot stove and this is the thanks I get?

- Bored! How can you be bored? I was never bored at your age.

- Go ask your dad. (Incidentally, when we did, he would defer back to my mom.)

- I used to walk to school uphill in the driving snow.

- I'll give you something to cry about.

- What part of NO don't you understand?

- You'll miss me when I'm gone one day, trust me.

- Don't make me pull this car over!

- I'm not asking you, I'm TELLING you.

- I don't care what the other kids' parents said, I said no.

The older we became, the funnier some of these sayings became. Yet, it was not so much the saying that caught our attention but the meaning behind them. Most of these simply translate into "you are my child and I want you to be safe from harm, think before you talk, and make good choices." Moms are special people and make a huge lasting impact on our lives. Their work ethic, caring and ability to multi-task provide great lessons for anyone in business. They are tireless, tolerant and seem indestructible; amazingly coming back for more each day.

Think about moms today and consider taking their lead when you go to work. Moms are pretty darn smart about life; it's instinctive and their shared lessons are more impressive than any business management book ever written.

Mom, thanks for all your lessons and sayings in the Perry household. Since you and other moms have the corner on the market for great one-liners, here is one for you from your three sons: WOW is MOM spelled upside down.

19

CTRL + ALT + DEL

———

Perhaps each year you make New Year's resolutions. They might include losing some weight, reading more, taking up a new hobby or spending more time with family. These may have appeared before as your New Year's resolutions, but for some reason they keep reappearing each year. Somehow, they just don't get accomplished. There are lots of reasons for New Year's resolution failure. We get busy, stuff happens, and we lose our focus and energy around these life enhancements.

We magically clean off last year's slate of experiences and look forward to the New Year with great optimism. That is the beauty of life: Even with its many twists and turns we take opportunities — like a new year — to renew, re-energize and get ready to get more out of our days.

For business owners and managers, there are new budgets, plans and strategies to prepare, which — with some luck and good timing — might work in our favor. We seek to get off to a fast

———

start in January so that our businesses are not playing catch up throughout the year. The holidays have passed, and in many parts of the country the weather stinks, unless you love cold, snow, slush and ice. Spring seems light years away. What a great time to get focused!

For employees, January can also represent a new beginning for their jobs or careers to be more fulfilling. Many have new performance expectations and goals to make greater contributions to their organizations. Business leaders are also challenged to enhance their work environments to help their employees meet and exceed performance expectations. Behavior changes on both ends may be in order to allow positive change to occur. The holiday break, along with the renewal of our calendar year, often permits both management and non-management employees a window of opportunity to think about work differently than they have in the past.

Even in high-performing, successful organizations there is always room for improvement. Becoming great is a process of continual improvement. The bar constantly rises in great organizations or in those that aspire to be the best. The task is pretty awesome, especially for organizations that just completed a record year. Encouraging employees at work to continuously meet and exceed expectations is not easy, especially in challenging economic and business conditions.

Over the years I have observed and experienced a simple formula for employee and organizational success. Attract and retain people who have a passion for their work and then provide them with an environment in which they can exceed their expectations. A long time ago, I quit trying to motivate people at work using monetary rewards, title changes, promotions or discipline. I realized that real motivation for employees to excel daily comes from within themselves.

For traditional managers this is a tough change from managing people using a carrot (rewards) or stick (discipline) approach to focusing on attracting and keeping high-performing employees and let them alone to do their jobs. Wonderful and surprising accomplishments occur when people at work are self-motivated and permitted to expand their horizons. It's great fun to watch people actually enjoy what they are doing, work with a passion and make their work-life fulfilling.

So as you embark on your next list of New Year's resolutions consider adding the following:

Talk With Your Top People: You already employ the best consultants for your business. Ask your top performers about your workplace practices, programs, compensation and benefits. What they have to say may shock you, and what they ask for may suggest significant changes to how you hire and employ people.

Make a Decision: Your organization's leadership should decide if it is prepared to embrace the concept of only hiring and keeping above-average performers. Recognizing that this is a process that won't happen overnight, the initiative if supported will yield a very different-looking workforce in just a few years. Your top people will be ecstatic that you are embarking on this mission and the poor performers will either enhance their performance or be weeded out over time.

Eliminate Policies: Top people typically do not like bureaucracy, restrictive policies or to be treated like children. Unfortunately too many organizations still retain policies that frustrate top performers. Traditional use-it-or-lose-it paid time off, restrictive bereavement policies and probationary periods are examples of polices that are archaic and nonsensical to your superstars. So why are you making them live with these programs?

Extreme Makeover: Take a walk around your facilities including your reception area, restrooms, employee dining areas and parking lot. Are you proud of the surroundings or are they as outdated as your HR policies? If "Battleship Grey" has graced your walls for years, consider new colors of paint. Check out employee work areas. Would you want to work there eight to ten hours per day? There are great upgrades to physical work environments that do not cost an arm and a leg. The investment you make will have a dramatic effect on your staff.

Well OK: If you have been straddling the fence on a wellness program for your employees, this should be the year you jump over that fence. Wellness and health education is not a fad. These programs work well for your employees and your bottom line. It can be as simple as a walking program at lunch, health risk assessments, getting rid of the junk in your vending machines or offering occasional health tips. It does not need to be a full-blown program to be effective. Regardless of what you do, optional wellness programs made available to your staff are appreciated and utilized, and the results can be impressive. You might even save a life.

Don't Manage: Traditional management styles do not fly with top-performing employees. Coach and lead rather than manage. If you have leaders in your organization who are traditional carrot-and-stick managers, change may be in order. This may be a very tough challenge, as you will be asking some of your top executives to get out of their comfort zone and operate differently. Top-performer acquisition and retention starts from the top. If it does not, expect anemic results.

A New Year means exciting possibilities for your organization. Consider some of these concepts and try them out for a year. You will have nothing to lose except some poor performers. For some leaders these are easy and common sense inclusions to their philosophy of developing a successful organization. In other organizations, they may be resolutions that will require not a New Year's resolution but rather a workplace revolution. In either case, commitment to these concepts can result in quantum leaps in business results.

The beginning of the year may be analogous to pressing the Ctrl + Alt + Del keys on your keyboard. This magical combination of keys restarts your computer and allows you to start anew. Think of this year as the time to focus on improving your business through things you can Control (Ctrl), seeking Alternatives (Alt) to the way you have always done things, and Deleting (Del) processes, staff and policies that are holding your businesses back. There has never been a better time than right now to re-boot personally and professionally. It's just a matter of pressing the right buttons.

20

SCARY WORKPLACES

For some employees, the make-believe haunted houses set up for Halloween are considered mild compared to where they go to work every day. There are still too many horror stories about employers and managers. With all the protection afforded to employees through current employment law and the need to hire qualified talent, one would think that undesirable workplaces would have been sent to the company graveyard many moons ago.

These scary workplaces are easy to spot. Employees are walking around like zombies — disengaged from their company and focused on living for the weekend. The financial performance of these companies reflects their weak human resources platform and high turnover among top performers. If you dare to enter these workplaces, here is what you might find:

Poor Working Conditions: From poor lighting to cramped unsanitary environments, some organizations have allowed their physical working conditions to deteriorate. These are places only a vampire would love — dark, dingy and drab colors that scream facility makeover.

Cobwebbed Policies: Too many organizations still have employment policies designed for poor performers, including use-it-or-lose-it vacation policies, archaic bereavement leaves and probationary periods. In essence, these are policies designed for employees who can't be trusted to work hard and be accountable and responsible. Managing poor-performing, disengaged employees is like blood getting sucked out of your company: Eventually it will kill the organization. If your company fits this model, perhaps it's time to drive a stake through the heart of your HR strategy, focusing instead on hiring and keeping people who truly drive organizational performance.

Bound to Work: When company priorities come before family, disaster looms, especially with top-performing employees. In this day and age, employees are seeking work environments that focus on work/life balance, wellness and family. Regardless of generation, the expectation of employers by employees is to support family and community activities outside of work that are meaningful and fulfilling.

Balls and Chains: Whether it is a glass ceiling or lack of organizational structure, workplaces that have artificial barriers to advancement are like nightmarish quicksand: If you don't move, you won't sink. Top performers who witness this type of environment are smart to make a quick exit before being caught up in the muck of discrimination, bureaucracy and lack of career planning.

Painful Process: Employment candidates are sometimes tortured with the lack of a professional response from companies taking too much time in the recruiting process. These days, candidates with great skill sets expect organizations to have their act together when recruiting for open positions. This includes appropriate and timely feedback to candidates, clear expectations regarding timing and process, and ease of application utilizing state-of-the-art technology solutions. Too much time kills deals and that is certainly true when recruiting top talent.

Train Wreck: When companies fail to support employee training, they slowly but surely cut off their ability to compete regionally, nationally and globally. It's as if an evil spell was cast on the company's leadership when they think that spending money on skill enhancement is a waste of corporate dollars. Unfortunately, this short-sided thinking is accelerating the company's demise.

No Guts: During the Great Recession it seemed there was a full moon out for two years. Some organizational leaders hid from making tough decisions until the big bad economy went away. The ripple effect with many company leaders worsened the economy, resulting in massive unemployment and decreased spending. This dug a grave almost too deep to escape from. Today, in spite of some economic relief, a few organizational leaders remain hidden and lack the courage to make critical decisions. Their strategy is "hope and wait." Top performers who witness this fear-based behavior in their organizations have or are in the process of making plans to exit, instead joining companies where there is true leadership.

Fortunately, these tales from the crypt are not the majority of companies out there. Even so, the weak links in any corporate community do not help a region get stronger. For all the companies that dispense with the old ways of running a business, you deserve applause. For those companies still stuck in the dark shadows of workplace tradition: Boo!

21

FOOD FIGHT!

If you work in an office setting, you likely receive annual notifications that the office refrigerator will be cleaned out by year-end. The alert is pretty direct: Any bags of food or food items not claimed by a certain date will be discarded.

This annual office ritual generates sighs of relief that the office refrigerator has some chance of being restored to its original clean state. The odors developed from food left for months will disappear, shelves will be emptied and cleaned and the fridge will be reset for another year of abuse.

In my travels to businesses near and far, it is interesting to hear the common issues surrounding this communal repository of food and the office kitchen. Here are a few of the stereotypical complaints and violations that permeate so many organizations:

Soaked: This may be one of the more grotesque sights at the office. This is the bowl left in the sink filled with water mixed with the remaining food from someone's breakfast, lunch or dinner.

The theory is that the oatmeal, soup or spaghetti sauce needs to soak in the bowl for an easier rinse in the future. The person who commits this kitchen crime leaves no evidence behind and remains seemingly anonymous, sometimes for years. The theory does end up working, as someone else is so disgusted with the soaking food in the sink that they end up rinsing it out and stacking it in the dishwasher.

Hit (the Button) and Run: A similar tactic is used by the person who microwaves their food, leaves a mess and then runs from the scene. If this behavior is repeated often enough, the microwave starts resembling a cave with stalactites growing from former microwaveable food items. Not a pleasant sight, and it results in people covering their food prior to microwaving it to avoid such food stalactites dripping into their meals. In some offices, these germ and mold-infested microwave ovens are so bad they cannot even be cleaned and have to be disposed of and replaced.

Freezer Burns: This is the classic food item left in the office freezer well past its prime. It has been there so long that it's actually become part of the freezer, resembling something out of the movie "Pirates of the Caribbean, Dead Man's Chest," where Davy Jones' crew were actually becoming part of his ship. The frozen box needs to be chiseled out of the freezer and then discarded quickly before someone decides to do the hit-and-run approach with it in the microwave.

Weekend Leftovers: Nothing compliments an office kitchen counter quite like employees' leftovers from their weekend bridal showers, birthdays and other special events. It's the food, dips, veggie trays, fruit trays and baked goods that got picked over by the employees' relatives and friends over the weekend. That employee doesn't want to let food go to waste that no one ate or wanted in the first place. Who knows how long this food sat out, how many children's hands touched it or how much double dipping took place. Yum, yum. Ironically, other employees hardly touch the stuff and it ends up getting tossed away at the end of the day anyway.

Aromatic Wonders: Some unique food items that employees cook can leave lingering odors not only in the kitchen, but also permeate the offices and hallways. When you walk in these particular organizations, you're not sure if you are in a restaurant or an office building. No one seems to complain, because evidently conversations about how food smells and looks are as taboo as conversations about sex, politics and religion at the office.

Scavengers: The ultimate office kitchen offense is taking someone else's food. Either the person taking the food sees something more appealing than what they brought to the office, or the weather is so bad outside they didn't want the hassle of going out to get their own meal. In either case, this one beats out all the other culinary office offenses combined.

No doubt that the office kitchen is an interesting place to be, prepare food and in some cases eat. Though it is all a part of working together in the same company, some of the stories I have heard are just hard to digest.

22

THE DATING GAME

———

Many years ago, there was a popular television program called *The Dating Game*. One lucky single man or woman would interview three single men or women. A wall divided the "interviewer" from the group of candidates, ensuring that selection would not be made based on looks alone. The interviewer would ask each of the three candidates straightforward questions that presumably would assist them with making the right choice for the perfect date.

At the end of a specific time period, the interviewer would be asked to choose between the three candidates. The two would finally meet face-to-face, then be whisked off to an exotic chaperoned vacation for two. It certainly was a fun television show, and enjoyed a 20-year run on the air.

Though the show was cancelled in 1986, the format of the program lives on in businesses every day: It's called recruitment and selection. This process has been refined for decades, yet

———

corporate recruitment and selection programs remain imperfect and full of risk. Even for organizations that employ the most sophisticated approaches to finding and hiring people, courtship does not always yield the perfect marriage.

Consider the many businesses that rely solely on interviewing as a way of identifying qualified candidates without additional information from background investigations, psychological assessments, pre-placement medical examinations and other tools. This approach could be crudely compared to getting married after a one-night stand — basing long-term, critical hiring decisions on very little information gathered during the recruitment process.

There may not be a foolproof system in place, but here are some ways to improve the probability that your hiring process will yield good candidates:

- Make sure there is a current job description for the open position and job expectations are defined.

- Have everyone on your interview team well versed with the requirements for the open position and the expectations for performance.

- Plan how you intend to attract qualified candidates for the opening and what criteria you will utilize to select the top candidates.

- Each person on your interview team should have specific information they will solicit from candidates and data they will share with candidates.

- Formulate interview questions that have a purpose. Asking

questions like "what are your strengths and weaknesses?" seldom provide sound data to support a hiring decision.

- Have a structure upon which selection results — like interview results — will be compared and evaluated.

- Treat all candidates fairly and share the selection process with each. In addition to interviews, utilize other selection tools that will yield critical information about candidates.

Perhaps it's time to assess your organization's recruitment and selection program. Is it consistently producing great candidates, or are you taking your chances on a process that is analogous to a "blind date?"

23

WILL YOU MARRY ME?

When newlyweds begin their lives together, there is great excitement, joy and the hope that this marriage thing works really well. The institution of marriage teaches us many lessons, regardless of whether you are an innocent bystander or a participant. Those with healthy long-term marriages provide us with a blueprint of how to successfully manage other legally binding partnerships like the traditional employer-and-employee relationship. Assuming your company is interested in attracting great candidates for long-term relationships — in other words, employment — here are a few ideas that might increase the probability that your marriage with them won't end in a nasty divorce.

Looking Good: Your company's image, personality and culture are critical in determining the type of employment candidates you attract. If you are known as an employer of choice for top-performing people, your chances increase dramatically that you will get the employees you have always dreamed about.

Online Dating: Today, having an online career center on your company's website and using social media for open positions are essential. Candidates of all ages are using the Internet to research companies, seek openings and learn about corporate cultures, compensation and benefit programs. Online career centers must be easy to navigate and impressive. If you do not have a web presence or your career center is archaic, good candidates may remove your company from consideration. You won't even get a chance for a first date.

The Courtship: If you are really serious about hiring top people with the intention of keeping them long term, ensure that your selection process is comprehensive. That includes developing an excellent and timely interview process, clarifying expectations, conducting a thorough background investigation and assessment testing. In addition, make sure candidates see where they will be "living" most of their waking hours and, most importantly, ensure they get to meet their future "family" of co-workers and managers. Last but not least, keep candidates in the loop regarding the process and timing. Their eyes can stray for a more attractive opportunity if you don't pay attention to them. If they have to ask where the relationship is going, you have not done your job.

Wedding Day: The big day is approaching when the selected candidate will become your employee and arrive for their first day on the job. Some planning needs to take place to ensure that new employees feel welcome and have the necessary tools and information to perform their jobs. Provide a directory of email addresses and phone extensions, have business cards ready and create a toolkit of office supplies and other basic workplace necessities ready for them. You might also want to plan a "reception" in the form of a lunch to welcome them.

The Honeymoon: Depending upon the organization, the honeymoon period with employees can last from a day to a few weeks. Typically, new employees enjoy a little time getting formally and informally oriented to the organization. Your orientation and on-boarding program should be personalized, consistent and well-rounded, providing opportunities for you and your new employee to warm up to each other and learn more about each other now that you are legally living together. Make sure this is an experience that reinforces their decision to work for your company.

Reality Sinks In: Once the excitement of the first few weeks has worn off, it will be critical to keep new employees engaged and interested. Like marriage, this can be a challenging time filled with lots of bumps along the way. There may be disagreements or concerns over compensation, budgets and other employees, plus questions about the direction of the company, job security, travel, expectations and workplace policies. Open lines of communication will be critical to manage through these issues. Keep the work challenging, fun and intellectually stimulating, especially for top-performing people. Understand your top performers' needs and be willing to address these along the way.

Show Appreciation: As time goes on, it's easy to take top performers for granted. That is dangerous territory, because top people are difficult to find and keep. Beyond your core recognition programs, consider surprising your top people now and then with recognition and rewards that wow them. They will appreciate the effort, and it will remind them that their partnership with you is a solid one. Last but not least, don't forget to commemorate their employment anniversary

Marriage is hard work at times and so is the employer-employee relationship. Many of your employees spend more time at work than with their significant others. Consider the elements of a successful marriage as you manage your workforce and chances are you'll have long-term employment relationships with some exceptional people.

24

FOR HEAVEN'S SAKE

———

There is an old joke that goes around every now and then about the afterlife. A deceased businessperson meets up with St. Peter and expresses excitement about entering heaven.

"Not so fast," St. Peter exclaims to the recently deceased. "You have a choice! Over the next two days you will be given a chance to visit both heaven and the underworld. Then you can decide where you want to spend eternity." The deceased raises an eyebrow at the obvious choice, but recognizes that the exercise is going to be necessary for entrance through the pearly gates.

The first visit is to the devil's place. To the deceased person's amazement, it is a delightful environment. Everyone looks terrific, including the devil. The food is spectacular, and after a round of sub-par golf with the devil, the deceased begins to see things differently than he had imagined. He wonders if this place might give heaven a run for its money. The next day, the deceased visits heaven. Angels are floating around playing harps with everyone apparently very happy. Heaven looks nice, but a bit boring to the deceased compared to the devil's underworld. Now it is decision time.

After much deliberation, the deceased businessperson makes a decision he never thought he would, choosing the devil's place over heaven. Upon hearing the decision, St. Peter clicks his fingers and the deceased arrives back in the underworld with the devil. This time, the scene is much different than the previous visit. Everything is gray, ugly and hot, and the devil is grotesque.

The deceased complains to the devil that this is not what had been presented on the first visit. The devil replies with a hideous smile, "The other day you were being recruited and today you are an employee. Welcome aboard!"

Do your new employees have a similar experience in their first few months of work at your company? If so, it might make sense to examine your company's existing recruitment and on-boarding process and programs. Here are a few ideas to consider:

Be Realistic: Ensure that your message about your company and the open position is consistent and accurate in all of your recruitment materials and orientation programs. This includes contents of your recruitment advertisements, online career center and discussions during the interview process.

No Surprises: Share information about your organization and open positions right from the start. For example, at the first interview, provide job candidates a copy of job descriptions, your company's performance review process and forms, performance expectations, organizational chart and key employment policies. In addition, an office or plant tour — including a walkthrough of where candidates would be physically working if selected — is a real plus.

Plan, Plan, Plan: A new employee's first day and week is a major event in their life. They are typically pretty nervous and want to make a good impression early. Yet the first week or so is often tough as the new employee is in unfamiliar surroundings and doesn't know very many people. Ensure that the first week is scheduled and that the new employee has the tools necessary to do their job. Having a buddy system also works wonders. Pairing a seasoned employee with a new employee in those first few weeks can work miracles and ensure that the new employee gets off to a great start.

Check In: After the first week, month and 90 days, check in with new employees. This follow-up will give you and the new employee an opportunity to ensure that things are going as planned. This approach also provides the employee confirmation that they likely made the right choice by accepting your offer of employment.

No Probation: If your company still has a probationary period for new employees, consider eliminating this archaic policy. It does nothing to support a positive new-hire start. Think about the message you're sending when a new employee learns that he or she will be on probation for the first 30, 60 or 90 days. Even the word probation has a negative connotation. Getting rid of this mixed-message policy can help get the employment experience off on the right foot.

Assess your organization's recruitment practices and employment policies. Ensure that they are designed to support top performer acquisition and retention. Provide a realistic view of your organization so that there are no surprises if they are hired. And for heaven's sake, consider eliminating policies like the probationary period that was designed as an easy out for poor hiring decisions.

Finding great people for your organization can be a real challenge. Increase your odds of bringing on and keeping some of the best performers in town by following solid, consistent, common-sense recruitment and retention programs and policies that work for you. If you do, you will provide another reason great employees will say your organization is "heaven-sent."

25

WANT TO TAKE A RIDE?

———————

I am inviting you to go on a great workplace journey with me. Here is what you need to pack: (1) unwavering commitment, (2) an open mind and (3) courage. Please leave traditional management thinking, policies and practices behind. They will weigh you down and prevent you from reaching the destination.

Whether or not you can make a successful trip depends upon your answer to the following question: "Is your organization committed to attracting and retaining only top performers?" Think of the answer to this question as your organizational Sherpa, your guide to business success. There is no right or wrong answer to the question. The key is to answer the question and communicate it to your entire staff. So if you are truly committed to only hiring and keeping good people, make sure everyone knows it. Likewise, if you are not, make sure all your employees know it — at least it will confirm what they see around your company.

———

If you're ready to take the trip toward establishing and maintaining a great workplace for top performers, then here are a few tips to follow along the way:

Define Them: Start with defining what characterizes top performers at your organization and in your various business units and support teams. You cannot even begin to attract and hire these people unless you know what you are seeking. This is a great management exercise: At your next team meeting, ask the participants to define top performer characteristics in your business. The answers will be interesting and may even surprise you.

Trust: This is critical to ensuring a successful journey. In order to thrive, your employees need to trust those in their workplace. It's easy to do with workplace superstars.

Compensation and Benefits: Top performers expect great pay and benefits. These are the free agents in business. They know it and expect to be well-compensated for what they bring to the table. If you are not committed to paying great people great pay, your trip is over.

Skinny Handbook: Remember that top performers dislike traditional employment practices and policies, especially archaic programs like use-it-or-lose-it vacation, bereavement leave, probationary periods and sick-time policies.

Performance vs. Time: Let top performers know what you expect, get out of the way and let them do their thing. It's all about measuring job performance, not time, for these people. If your organization believes that hours worked measure employee loyalty or work performance, you are wasting your time on this trip.

Recruitment and Selection: Organize your recruitment and selection strategy around attracting top people and increasing the probability they will work in your business. This approach goes way beyond traditional hiring approaches and encourages creative ways to get top performers' attention. From social media to employee referrals to targeted networking, today's savvy top workplaces are designing recruiting and selection game plans that bypass average performers and raise the collective eyebrow of those people who can come into the business and make a big difference. It's all about a positive workplace brand that creates a following among the best in the business.

Just Like Me: Top performers want to work with other top performers. The greater your top performer population, the greater the chance you can attract and keep other top people.

If you believe that most of your organization's success and growth can be attributed to your best people, then this trip is for you. Make the journey to develop and enhance your workplace for top performers; it's worth the time and extra effort, and your employees and business will benefit in production and in workplace culture.

Great workplaces also recognize that the journey to a great workplace for top people never ends. Top performers strive for continuous process improvement and are not content with the status quo. That is a good thing if you and your leadership team feel the same way.

26

KIDS THESE DAYS

"I see no hope for the future of our people if they are dependent on the frivolous youth of today, for certainly all youth are reckless beyond words. When I was a boy, we were taught to be discreet and respectful of elders, but the present youth are exceedingly wise and impatient of restraint."

Though you might believe this statement is true today, it actually dates back to the ancient Greek poet Hesiod in 700 BC. In present day, we have a unique anomaly occurring — there are four distinct generations working together and another one on the way. These include Veterans, Baby Boomers, Generation X, Millennials and soon to follow, what some are referring to as Generation Z.

If you have an organization where a few or all of these groups are represented, you know their generational differences can cause raised eyebrows among co-workers. Those differences can also result in a multitude of communication, morale, HR policy, compensation, recruitment and retention issues. Writer George Orwell may have said it best: "Every generation imagines itself to be more intelligent than the one that went before it, and wiser than the one that comes after it."

Some organizations are fighting this cultural diversity, while others embrace and welcome the change and challenges the multiple generations bring to the table. The latter organizations will come out as clear winners in the long run, while traditional organizations that attempt to homogenize their workforce will find top performers exiting quickly to greener pastures.

Here are few practical steps to consider if you have a few or more generations represented among your people:

Assess Your Employee Demographics: Begin with a look at your workforce from the perspective of the generational groups highlighted above. At the risk of being stereotypical, it is a pretty good place to start and provides you with a base of knowledge of strategies you may need in the future.

Train Your Management Team: From first-line supervisors to the CEO, your management team needs to understand that age and background can explain some of the behaviors exhibited in their departments. They must upgrade their skill sets in managing multiple generations while supporting the attraction and retention of top performers.

Assess Recruiting Practices: Assuming your goal is to attract the best talent available, it will be necessary to recognize that one size does not fit all when it comes to recruiting. Placing a classified ad in the newspaper may work to attract a Baby Boomer, but not a Millennial candidate who searches for jobs online. Spend some time looking at your most successful sourcing tools and continue to ask top employees across the generations where their peers are finding jobs.

Assess Policies and Benefits: Retaining top performers across the generations can also be a difficult task. It can no longer be a one-dimensional approach but one that mandates an appreciation for what people are seeking in a great workplace. Ask your top people across the generations why they stay at your organization. Their honest and direct feedback can provide an excellent blueprint for future policies, work environment considerations and employee benefits.

Generational differences can either be looked at with disdain or as a welcome challenge. On occasion I hear Baby Boomers complain about the young people in their workplaces with statements like "They don't have a work ethic," or "they want to run our company without paying their dues." I am not sure why there is so much concern. It is not like the Veterans or Boomers perfected the workplace. The upcoming generations are inheriting some archaic HR policies and programs, along with gender differences in pay, corruption in corporate America and glass ceilings, just to name a few.

There is hope for upcoming generations to have an opportunity to turn a real mess around. They can do better — much better. They can be the greatest generation for corporate America. And that's not something to kid about.

27

FAMILY FIRST

———————

It's hard for me to believe that it has been over a decade since my dad's battle with cancer came to an end. Over the last months of his life, I remember how important it was for me to have support at work so I could have the time I needed to be with my dad. I remember thinking how lucky I was to work in an environment where family came first. Because of my staff, I was able to spend quality time with my dad and family without guilt or pressure from work. It made a huge difference during a very difficult time.

That's why it is never a surprise when I see employee survey results that reflect that workers rank work-life balance at or near the top of the most important job attributes when seeking and staying at a job. These days, employees expect employers to support a balance between work and family.

Though there are laws like the Family Medical Leave Act mandating certain leave provisions for employees, family-friendly workplaces are often characterized as organizations that go well beyond state and federal employment law to support workers' family needs, desires and obligations.

In addition to family-friendly workplaces, the phrase work-life balance is used as another descriptor related to employees' management of personal and work obligations. As these concepts have gained momentum, employers are faced with the challenge of supporting employees' family and personal needs and obligations. It's a tough balancing act for both employee and employer, but when both parties' needs are met the results are impressive. Here are a few thoughts and ideas to consider when assessing your organization's support of family-friendly workplace initiatives:

Do You Care? Like other HR programs and policies, the first step is to assess management's commitment. Is the organization willing to pursue a family-first environment and philosophy instead of remaining a work-first company? A family-first workplace relies on trust as the critical component of the program because many of these employment policies allow employees significant flexibility, self-accountability and possibly time away from work. With trust being such an important factor in family-friendly environments, it is not surprising that these companies also aspire to the philosophy of attracting and retaining only top people.

Is It Believable? Perception is reality when it comes to a family-friendly workplace. Employees must see that family-friendly policies and programs are consistently supported without resistance or retaliation by management and supervisors. Employees should be able to take advantage of such programs and policies without fearing they will lose their jobs or diminish long-term career opportunities. Either commit to doing it right with the proper support, or don't even bother.

What should we implement? The benefits, policies, and programs of a family-friendly workplace are the most visible aspects of a program. There is a wide array of choices including:

Flexible Work Options: These include programs like working at home, compressed work weeks, part-time work, job sharing and flexible scheduling. Though options may require some job re-design, it is worth the effort if it allows you to retain a top-performing employee.

Family and Personal Leaves: Programs required by law are a must, but consider going even further than state and federal mandates.

Education: Workshops and seminars relative to financial planning, work-life planning, college aid, elder care, advance directives and a host of other personal or family-related topics provide employees with great information, save tons of time and reduce stress related to these issues.

Child Care or Elder Care Programs: Consider offering on-site or off-site daycare, referrals, subsidies and after-school or summer programs.

Non-traditional Benefits: Beyond a strong standard compensation and benefits package, more companies are adding family-friendly benefits like long-term care insurance, financial planning, wellness programs, a comprehensive Employee Assistance Program, short and long-term disability coverage, and other unique programs like pet insurance (Yes, Fido is considered to be part of the family).

Concierge Services: Convenience services like drop-off dry-cleaning are quickly becoming an important part of family-friendly workplaces. These services are appreciated by staff and provide precious time savings for day-to-day tasks.

Employment Policies: Replace archaic use-it-or-lose-it sick and vacation policies with paid time-off programs that allow employees to manage their schedule responsibly. Top-performing employees dislike traditional employment policies and appreciate being treated like adults. In addition, establish a bereavement leave policy that allows employees to come back to work following the loss of a loved one when they are good and ready.

Recognition: Recognition polices are being expanded beyond employees at work to their families. Employers are increasingly showing their appreciation of families' support at home for employees' hard work and performance.

Today, the pressures on employees and their families have increased significantly due to the challenging economy, especially in cases where one spouse is working while the other seeks new employment. The ripple effect on child care, elder care, financial and physical health can create issues that the workplace has not seen in quite some time. Likewise, pressures on employers have increased dramatically to succeed in this new era. A perfect storm has been created where employers need more top-performing employees and those employees need more support at their workplaces.

The conditions are right to assess your organization's approach to top-performer attraction and retention. Consider providing more support to employees who are responsible for driving most of your organizational results. Now is the perfect time to dump traditional approaches to business and invest in progressive HR systems and polices that create an environment where top people flourish.

It's a great opportunity to move your business forward while making a difference at home.

28

WHY FAILURE IS SO CRITICAL TO BUSINESS SUCCESS

I discovered a long time ago that not much is learned from success. It's not success but failures that really make a difference in our world. They shape our perspective and provide guidance on how to do things better and smarter.

There is so much emphasis on success in business that we often forget how it actually gets achieved. Success just does not happen, it's not easy and it comes along with plenty of frustration, anxiety and sometimes tears. Show me a successful businessperson and I will show you someone who most likely failed quite a bit during his or her career journey.

In this age of instant gratification, it is not surprising that instant success in business seems to be expected. Unfortunately, as nice as instant success would be, it's trial and error that is the foundation of business progress.

If you really want to see more innovation at your organization and more successful outcomes, consider re-wiring your perspective on failure. It may sound crazy, but here are some ideas on how to increase the probability of failure:

Start at the Top: Corporate leaders usually ascend to their positions through careers filled with accomplishments, which are most likely backed by years of starts and stops, risk-taking and failures. With this knowledge, great leaders work on sustaining work environments that support employees who stick their neck out, fall short a few times, brush themselves off and pursue excellence. Companies known for innovation have these environments where top performers thrive.

Establish a Failure Reward Program: This may sound wacky, but it works. It's the opposite of how people are trained to think, and yet rewarding trial and error has a greater longer-term impact on your workforce than short-term rewards for success. And rewards do not need to be monetary. Often, public praise for the effort and next steps shows other employees that continuous process improvement is rewarded rather than simply the end result. It is all about improving and adjusting each day, which means plenty of failures along the way. Focus on the process and experience and the success will follow.

Hire the Right People: In order for innovation to occur, you need people on your staff who love stretching their minds and skill sets. These are the people who often drive organizational results. In the right work environment, risk-taking, innovative high achievers make magic happen. A couple of failures along the way for these top performers are simply benchmarks to them, not roadblocks.

Don't Fail to Ask: Have individual, small and large group conversations about failure. Gain a perspective on what your employees' thoughts are on the subject and if they feel your work setting supports the process or only the result. The best "consultants" you can access are your employees. So spend time with them to have open dialogue on the subject of failure. It will be eye opening. And listening to their views, fears and interests on the subject of failure will be eye opening for you too!

Failure is all about learning how to handle adversity and getting better. Failure teaches us life-long lessons, many of which we should apply in and outside of work. The most important of all these, I believe, is that "failing to fail will certainly result in failure."

29

TIME TO GET BOARD

———————

Most organizations have a board of advisors or directors who help support the growth and success of the business. Ideally, board members provide objective perspectives, advice and direction to an organization's leadership.

If an organization has the right composition and expectations are well-defined, its board can play a key role in developing sound strategy, helping with decision-making and supporting business success. Effective boards require time and energy to develop and are contingent on selecting great fits for different board positions.

Just as your organization utilizes outside counsel to assist with its success, consider your own personal "board of advisors" for personal and professional success. You may already have some of these board members in place without realizing it:

Health and Wellness: Your doctor and dentist are already part of your "advisory" team. They represent the medical expertise of your board and play a critical role in your lifelong success. In addition, identifying individuals with expertise with diet, stress management and fitness can also complement your health and wellness team.

Legal Affairs: Utilizing a trusted attorney is essential for ensuring that you have all the legal documents that will protect your assets and provide guidance to your loved ones in the event of your death or disability. An attorney also provides great advice on many of the legal documents you are asked to sign along your life's journey, such as major purchases, employment agreements and miscellaneous contracts.

Money Matters: Having a qualified financial planner provide guidance on how to manage and invest your hard-earned dollars can be very important in these volatile economic times and market conditions. From prudent budgeting to retirement planning, good financial planners can make a world of difference on how well your money can work for you and your family. They can help you establish a game plan for wealth accumulation and quickly decipher the right investment choices given your risk tolerance and life situation.

Taxes: Tax forms and tax planning seem to get more complicated each year. Making sure that your tax returns are accurate and complete may require using an outside professional, depending upon your circumstances. In addition, utilizing outside counsel to assist in the best approach to tax strategies throughout the year can save you a ton of money.

Risk Management: Whether it is your automobile, home or possessions, utilizing a licensed professional to assist with assessing your risks and potential liabilities is critical in protecting all that you have worked so hard to own. In addition, understanding your needs and coverage levels for health, life, disability and long-term care insurance ensures you have the right protection for your life situation.

Career: Typical careers span an average of 40 to 45 years. That is a heck of a lot of time, so you might as well know, believe and love what you are doing. Some people struggle to identify a great job and then secure the position. For those who are challenged with finding that perfect job, using a career coach might be the answer. They can provide an objective assessment of your skill sets, experience and interests and be of great help in moving you toward career happiness.

Family: Don't overlook one of the best individuals around to be part of your personal board — your significant other. He or she cares about you, is (hopefully) a good listener and has your best interests at heart. Your significant other will most likely need to be involved in understanding the assistance and information you receive from your other personal board members.

Emulate the business model by securing a credible and knowledgeable board of advisors for yourself. It can be an incredibly smart move that pays dividends in the short and long term. Interestingly, top performers at work are typically also top performers in their personal life; people with a high achievement orientation often surround themselves with winners.

Consider taking a few moments to think about your own board of advisors. Do you have the right people in place? Are they doing a great job for you? Having the right team in place can make a world of difference in how successful you can be in and outside of work. Taking on life alone is a tough road, so consider having the right team of experts to help you with the journey. So, when you get to those forks in the road, chances are your board can point you in the right direction.

30

YOU DON'T SAY

One sign of an organization's health is the ability of employees at all levels to share their thoughts, ideas and opinions openly and honestly with upper management. Companies that support open communication find that employees and their businesses are significantly more successful in virtually every aspect of day-to-day operations. These companies are really cool places to work, places where risk-taking is encouraged and — not surprisingly — innovation is widespread.

Unfortunately, too many workplaces are infected with bureaucracy, politics, fear and game-playing, which creates an environment where anonymity provides the only avenue for freedom of speech. It's a sad scenario and one that creates a work environment full of fear, deception and finger-pointing.

Make no mistake, most employees would love to have a positive say in the business in which they work. And there is no one that knows your business better than the people who work there day-to-day. Tapping into the collective experience of your staff is smart business and is a critical element of your company's success. Here are a few ideas to help open up communication in your company:

It Starts at the Top: If you are an organizational leader, have you created an environment of trust and respect in your workplace? If people fear you or are intimidated by you, your organization does not have a chance to maximize its potential. People will hold back, including the management team that surrounds you. Spend more time walking around your company and engaging employees in thoughtful conversation. It will take time, but if you genuinely listen to employees you will soon see people opening up to you like never before. And you will be leading by example, prompting your management team to follow suit.

Staff Meetings: Encourage people to speak up at staff meetings. If they do, don't blow their ideas out of the water. If you do squash ideas, there is little likelihood those employees will ever offer up suggestions or feedback again. It will also send a signal to others that it is safer to be quiet than to ruffle the feathers of the company's leadership.

Eliminate Anonymity: If you need to have employees provide feedback anonymously then you have a heck of a lot of work to do in opening up communication lines and reducing the fear factor. Whether it is a suggestion box or an employee opinion or engagement survey, your goal should be to have employees participate enthusiastically without the need for anonymity.

Performance Reviews: Your management team should be well-versed and trained in the art and science of providing performance reviews and coaching. They need to follow your lead and provide timely, open and honest dialogue with employees about their performance — both good and bad. Companies that have an environment of open communication provide ongoing feedback to employees throughout the year, rather than waiting for the traditional once-a-year formal performance review.

Give Credit Where Credit is Due: Ensure that you are publicly praising and rewarding employees who provide great ideas that benefit the company. It sends a wonderful, powerful and positive message to the staff that ideas are welcome and encouraged.

It Starts With Interviews: Make sure candidates for open positions understand that employees are encouraged and expected to be active participants in the success of the organization. Ideas should be welcome and encouraged.

Hire and Keep the Right People: Work hard at identifying the very best people for open positions and focus on retaining the employees who drive 100 percent of your organization's results. Keeping employees with poor attitudes about themselves and their work will hold you back, negatively affecting open communications and discouraging the type of positive workplace you seek.

There are many more ways to support open communication with your entire staff. It takes a lot of work and happens over time. In an era where so many people hide behind electronic communications and social media, it can be challenging to maintain a high level of interpersonal communication at your organization. Yet, if you are successful, you will find that you will no longer have to ask employees to share their ideas anonymously, nor will you have to wonder what your people are thinking.

31

HR: THE NEW MARKETING DEPARTMENT

———————

Recently, a friend in the midst of a career transition vented to me that employers were not returning her calls following interviews or responding to résumé submissions. Her frustration is shared by many who have found that a buyers' market for job candidates can translate into a lack of response from many employers. Make no mistake, job candidates do not forget these communication lapses by employers. They remember the good, bad and ugly. Employers who mess up with job candidates today forget that these folks are consumers, potential future clients and possibly their future boss.

The hiring process is but one example of how impactful the HR process and communication systems are when it comes to a company's image in the business community and general public. Current employees also represent a critical lifeline for your organization's continued sales success and image as a great company and employer of choice. Given today's challenging business climate, there is an opportunity for HR to play a much larger role in external and internal marketing and promotion.

Consider the following opportunities where HR can support your company's positive image and reputation inside and outside of the organization:

Recruiting: Whether it's an online local job posting or a print classified advertisement, ensure that your organization's open positions stand out. Get rid of boring ads that candidates will skim right past. Provide an easy way for candidates to apply and confirm your receipt of their information even if their qualifications are nowhere near a match for your openings. Timing is everything, so processes should ensure quick responses and provide candidates with direction on possible next steps.

Also, look at the recruiting process as an opportunity to recruit new customers. Let's say your organization is a local retailer. Along with your confirmation of their résumé, email information about your stores and provide candidates a coupon for a significant percentage off their next purchase. Remember, you are only hiring one person per opening and you likely had 50 to 100-plus apply. Work on developing customer relationships with applicants who did not get the job. If you treat applicants poorly, don't expect them to be fans of your stores. They have plenty of choices to shop, so work on increasing the probability that they will think kindly of your organization. Goodwill is more powerful than any advertising.

Interviewing: Interviews are an extraordinary face-to-face opportunity to present your organization in a positive light. Provide candidates with takeaways that will serve as reminders of their good experience with you and your team. Be organized, respect their time and treat them like gold. Provide candidates an explanation of the process and what they should expect next. Don't forget an office or plant tour and, if possible, give a nice gift as a token of appreciation for their time. Candidates not selected for the position are more likely to think well of your company if they enjoyed a positive experience during this phase of the selection process.

Stage Presence: Your company's HR team is always on stage. From the moment your HR staff pull into your company's parking lot, they are being observed and judged by other employees. The HR staff's dress, conversations, written correspondence, presentations and adherence to company policies all translate into a level of credibility for the rest of your employees. Therefore, the pressure is on for HR professionals to lead by example so that their credibility is high. It is a critical element of their success in gaining buy-in on new programs, policies and employment-related initiatives. It is also HR's leadership that helps facilitate workplaces that evolve into employers of choice for top performers. There is no doubt that your HR team's performance plays a direct and critical role in building your corporate image. It can either support or dilute your company's marketing initiatives and promotions.

Image is Everything: I was recently driving down the interstate and spotted a cleaning company's van that was caked with dirt. I laughed at the irony and wondered if the business owner was aware that his company's "music and dance" were not in sync. The same goes for your company's physical working conditions, office and plant layout, company vehicles and even HR forms. All of these send a message to employees, customers, prospective customers and job candidates. HR can take the lead role in improving the message you're sending to ensure that a consistent, high-quality and positive image of your company is on display within and outside of the organization.

Sales Staff: Every person who works in your organization is your company representative. How employees perform and interact, within and outside of your organization, is a direct reflection on what your company stands for. HR's role, with top management's support, is to lead with an aggressive passion for developing and maintaining a workplace that attracts and retains top performers, who can become great ambassadors for your organization. There is no marketing program on earth that can beat out the impact a top-performing staff can have on growing your business.

If HR is not directly involved with your marketing staff, now is the time to get them together and start the dialogue. The possibilities are exciting. And, more importantly, my friend and many other job candidates will really appreciate hearing back from you.

32

DO YOU RECOGNIZE ME?

Mary Kay Ash, founder of Mary Kay Cosmetics, may have put it best when she said, "There are two things people want more than sex and money — recognition and praise." This is a really thought-provoking insight. It's ironic how the driver behind a company that specializes in enhancing outer beauty knew that the really important stuff was underneath the skin.

Magic happens when people are recognized. It's magic because the response to heart-felt, genuine recognition can't be seen most of the time. Yet it may be the most powerful element of psychological sustenance on earth.

Today, top workplaces provide employee recognition that goes well beyond congratulating good job performance and years of service. Many organizations acknowledge employees in a variety of ways for life events, exceptional effort, community service, "wow" customer service, risk-taking, new ideas, extended business travel and even failure. How employees are recognized goes well beyond the traditional performance review, pay raise, promotion or gift.

Step back and take a look at the elements of your organization's employee recognition efforts. Here are a couple of items to consider adding to the mix:

Celebrate 11 Years: Why do we only seem to celebrate employment anniversaries in increments of five years? Shouldn't we make a bigger deal out of six years than five and 11 years over ten, and so on? Each year is a big deal, and it is worth enhanced celebration, especially for your top people who have stuck with you.

Surprise! Unexpected positive recognition is a great way to wow your employees. It makes the message loud and clear that you do not take employees for granted. I guarantee that you will make their day.

Family Affair: The families behind your employees are an essential part of your organization. They provide a critical support system for your staff and at times make sacrifices at home when your employees work long hours, travel on business or are working on a particularly challenging project. Don't forget them; employees' families are your extended team.

The Baggage is Full: Everyone has personal baggage, and though corporate America mandates that staff leave it at the door, it is impossible to shed. Most people keep their personal pain under wraps at the workplace, but it's still there. Acknowledge this reality and recognize that some people have bad days for reasons well outside of work. Appreciate it and support them when you can.

Thump, Thump: Employee recognition should be done for the right reasons. It should not be an obligation or a chore. Giving acknowledgement should be fun and from the heart. If you can't genuinely recognize employees, don't fake it. That's worse than not acknowledging them at all.

Daily Exercise: Ask every one of your employees to make a commitment to making a difference in someone's life every day. Large or small, daily acts of kindness, acknowledgement and recognition can be game-changers for recipients.

There are a million ways to recognize employees. Just search "employee recognition" on the Internet, and the ideas will be limitless. Be creative, have fun and remember that we pay these great people to show up every day and work hard. They do not owe us, we owe them.

We also know that the no-cost, easiest and least-used form of recognition is looking someone in the eyes and saying "thank you." Start there and watch the magic unfold.

33

REVIEW YOUR REVIEWS

It is the rare manager or non-management employee that relishes the employee performance review process. Most of us were not really built to be the judge and jury mandated during this annual, quarterly and/or monthly endeavor. In some cases, managers get so worked up over giving performance reviews they become physically ill.

Perhaps some of the anxiety, distress and disdain related to performance reviews fall into one or more of the following categories:

Timing: Many formal performance reviews are still performed on an annual basis, which can cause dissatisfaction among employees who wish for more frequent two-way communication of their performance throughout the year.

Procrastination: Some managers have been accused of waiting until the annual performance review process to provide meaningful feedback to their employees. Often, procrastination of sharing tough news can yield disastrous results, including workplace violence.

Save the Date: Managers that consistently reschedule performance reviews with their employees are sending a message to their staff that they are unimportant.

The Form: Sometimes the form utilized during performance reviews can actually restrict open dialogue with the form itself driving the process. It should be the other way around. A one-size-fits-all performance review form seldom results in meaningful reviews.

Training: A lack of experience or training among managers who provide reviews can also spell disaster.

Necessary Evil: Some managers look at the performance review as an HR administrative mandate rather than a constructive discussion between two parties. This poor attitude can only hurt the process and is unfair to the receiving party.

Absence of Expectations: You can't measure performance if you have nothing to measure it against.

If any of these issues are familiar, think about re-tooling your approach by considering the following:

Makeover: Throw out the status quo and start anew. A great place to begin is by asking your top performers to help design a program that makes sense for them and the organization. Don't be surprised if your elite performers tell you that they don't want a formal program. These are the same people who don't like to be managed, read employee handbooks, deal with policies and bureaucracy. They just want to excel at their jobs.

Hire Top Performers: Discussion of performance expectations begins in the interview process and not on the employee's first day of employment. Identify top performers, hire top performers and let them know what you expect. They will exceed your expectations most of the time.

Informality: Though we have all been taught to document every step we take at the workplace, consider more frequent conversations without having the written formality of an official form. Top performers like to know where they stand all the time, not just once a year.

Starts at the Top: If you are the CEO, you know it starts from the top. Be a champion and cheerleader for outstanding performance management. Lead by example and watch productivity improve in your organization.

Keep it Simple: Most of all, don't let the formality of the process of reviewing an employee's performance get in the way of a great conversation. It's a simple concept that we have made complicated, clumsy and archaic over time.

The critical component of an organization's performance review program is whom you hire and whom you keep. Hire and keep average to below-average employees and you end up with an annual disciplinary process versus constructive dialogue about performance. If you attract and retain top performers — and over time weed out the poor performers — you will liberate your organization from dysfunctional and hated performance reviews. Now that will be a performance worthy of a great review.

34

LET'S TALK

The other night, while out to dinner with my family, another family a few tables down from us caught my attention. The parents and two children were each on their smartphones, engrossed in whatever activity was taking place on their respective devices. Throughout their entire dinner, they remained fixated on their individual smartphone activity. As I looked around the restaurant I realized how many other people were dividing their attention between their companions and their smartphones.

In fact, in just about any place where people congregate, smartphone addiction seems to be the rule rather than the exception. Unfortunately this also includes too many drivers who believe they can operate a motor vehicle expertly while texting.

At business events and meetings, more and more attendees are routinely accessing their messages and managing information on their smartphones, rather than paying attention to the meeting or event speaker. Today, it is not uncommon to attend a business meeting and see at least half of the attendees place their smartphones on the conference room table. In years past, this was considered rude behavior, but somehow it has become acceptable. More than a few HR professionals have also shared with me that some job applicants are actually bringing their smartphones into interviews and answering text messages while being interviewed!

These are just a few examples of the smartphone addiction epidemic sweeping our globe and business world. If you are irritated with others due to their smartphone-addicted behaviors at work, events and business meetings, you may be classified as being "out of touch" or "behind the times."

Sadly, the art of conversation, developing business relationships and engaging in human interaction appears to be dying. The increasing attraction and dependence on electronic communication is easy to understand, because it is simple, fast and convenient. Yet in so many instances the true content and context of the intended message gets lost in cyberspace. This can lead to misinterpretations and breakdowns in communication.

It's not just an irritation. Smartphone abuse is destroying the following critical skill sets necessary for short and long-term personal career and business success:

Verbal and Written Communication: No matter how advanced technology becomes, the ability to effectively convey thoughts verbally and in writing — that doesn't include texting — will continue to be essential to your success. If you are doubtful, just try to upgrade your career opportunities based on good looks and exceptional texting skills.

Critical Conversations: In business, there are tough decisions that need to be made, and these often require difficult conversations. There is no hiding behind a screen to convey messages to individuals and employee teams. It needs to be done in person, in a timely fashion and with great preparation.

Public Presentation Skills: If you want to succeed in most business positions, you have to develop above average public presentation skills, backed by expertise.

Professional Network: If you believe that social media is the answer to developing a solid network of business professionals, you are sadly mistaken. In the real world, business is done with people where in-person, authentic relationships and trust have been established. Business professional credibility is not established online. In fact, it's through some social media avenues that careers and credibility have been destroyed because of posts or pictures that display poor judgment.

If you find yourself admitting that you might have the smartphone bug during working hours, turn your phone off. If it's critical for you to check messages, do it during your personal breaks or lunchtime. You will find yourself becoming more productive, more focused and more considerate of co-workers and your boss. Last but not least, respect people giving presentations publicly and leave your smartphone turned off or in your car.

These changes in behavior may be extremely difficult at first. But you may feel liberated once you get back to working without the smartphone seemingly attached to your hand. Ironically, people are corresponding more than ever because of technology, yet losing one of our most human attributes, which is the ability to effectively communicate face-to-face.

In the workplace, good communication is still an essential ingredient to success, teamwork and morale. If you or members of your staff are electronic communication addicts and believe that good business still relies on excellent communication, here are a few ways to break the habit:

Meetings: Consider banning all electronic devices from your business meetings. Don't be surprised if you get some nasty looks, since you're asking attendees to stow away their electronic crutches temporarily. You may find that attendees participate more in the discussion, are more focused and actually listen to the discussions. Plus you will have eliminated the occasional phone call that comes through on a phone that was not turned to the vibrate setting.

Sales Calls and Trade Shows: Ask your salespeople to leave their electronic devices in their cars or completely shut them off prior to walking into a customer or prospective customer's building. It can be pretty annoying greeting a salesperson in your reception area who is fixated on their smartphone, laptop or tablet. Even worse is the salesperson's pitch in the sales meeting being interrupted by an incoming message or a call coming through on their smartphone. Re-train your salespeople to prepare for their greetings and meetings with electronic devices off.

Have you been to a trade show lately? Watch how many exhibitors are sitting at their booths emailing, texting or tweeting instead of standing up, meeting, greeting and engaging others in conversation. If your organization exhibits at trade shows, request that your company's trade show representatives only check their electronic devices in private and on breaks. Then arrive at the show unannounced and check out how well your company is being represented.

Reception and Your Workforce: Think of your company's

reception desk as your permanent trade show booth. If you have frequent visitors that tour your company, recognize that all of your employees and their activities are on display to guests and prospective customers. Consider mandating that personal electronic devices be accessed only on breaks for anyone covering the reception area. Remember you are paying employees to work for your business rather than working on collecting friends on Facebook.

Parting Thoughts: There was a time when we got to know a great deal about people without relying on social media. It was a different time, that's for sure. There will be no turning back, and that's a shame. Today we have information coming at us at lightning speed with little ability to manage all of it. Our culture has evolved to being a bunch of isolated button-pushers using electronics to work, buy, play, date, communicate, eat and live. In the name of speed we have sacrificed our most precious attribute: the ability to be truly human.

In business, making a positive impression at work and with customers has always been an essential element of success. Yet all the convenience of electronic communication leaves everyone making no impression. So try something different to make that positive and lasting impression: Pick up the phone to respond to an email message rather than shooting off a quick electronic reply. Write three to five thank-you notes by hand to customers. It might take a few extra minutes and a bit more energy, but what you will find is a refreshing departure from the norm and the first steps to truly communicating.

Ironically, technology designed to bring us all closer together has made us more distant. Yet, there is one button on our handheld devices that can save us and get us back to basics at work and at home. It's called the OFF button. If we don't use it more often, smartphones will continue to turn us into dumb people.

35

MIRROR, MIRROR ON THE WALL

—————

Many years ago I participated in a physical conditioning course. The trainer, who was the picture of health, made us work very hard during each session with some of the toughest workouts I ever experienced. Talk about pain!

After each workout, the trainer provided us tips on staying in shape. He promised to get us in the best shape of our lives, but it would be up to us to stay there. During the final class, he sat us all down and reminded us (again) that physical fitness was a life-long endeavor and that we needed to remain committed to a program of continuous improvement.

During this final session, he really caught our attention when he shared one of his secrets to life-long fitness success. Anytime he found himself straying from his exercise routine and healthy diet he would stand in front of a full-length mirror — without clothes on! This unique approach provided plenty of motivation, he said, especially if he did not like what he saw.

He went on to tell us that while the scale was most others' measurement for fitness success, it seldom told the whole story. The mirror, he concluded, was the world's great performance measurement tool when it came to being physically fit. He cautioned that the use of the medicine chest mirror was only telling a part of the story; true success is measured by looking at the whole body with the lights on using a full-length mirror. With that, he wished us luck and good health.

We all know plenty of organizations that look great on the outside. They have nice commercials, positive media coverage, colorful advertisements, a cool website, awards and executives who rise to the level of celebrity status. For some, these are the measurements of success — the good-looking "clothes" that organizations wear.

Yet what happens when you disrobe organizations of their outerwear and take a look from top to bottom? Now and then, you may want to turn on the lights really bright and look at your organization objectively to see if the music really does match the dance. Stepping back and objectively assessing your organization's corporate fitness can sometimes be challenging and might not be very pretty. You may find that you want to put those organizational clothes back on pretty quickly after taking a look.

If your organization is willing to look in the mirror, consider the following in your assessment:

Top Performers: Does your organization have the practices, policies, programs and benefits necessary to attract, retain and motivate top performers? Is your organization committed to hiring and keeping the best?

Working Conditions: Are employees provided a safe, clean work environment that supports their personal and organizational success?

Workplace Policies: Are your policies up to date? Do they reflect a progressive workplace environment that stimulates creativity, innovation, risk-taking and productivity?

Technology: Has your organization embraced technology and leveraged existing applications to gain a competitive edge?

Recruitment: Do your recruitment programs focus on top-performer acquisition? Have you invested in an online career center to support these endeavors?

Reward Systems: Does your company provide cash and non-cash awards for exceptional work?

Disaster Recovery: Is your organization ready for the unforeseen?

Leadership: Are the right people employed in managerial positions and do they lead by example?

Sales Force: Does the organization rely solely on paid salespeople to stimulate revenue growth, or does it expect every employee to serve as a salesperson for the organization?

Bureaucracy: Are systems in place with the right organizational design to allow effective decision-making, risk-taking and creative thought?

Community Involvement: Does the organization support employees' community and civic efforts through donations or non-monetary support?

Pride: Are employees proud to work for your organization?

Ethics: Does the organization conduct its business with the highest ethical standards guiding its path?

Like the Cinderella story, when you look in the organizational mirror do you want it to tell you something that may not be true or do you want an honest assessment? Perhaps you want to be the fairest of them all, and perhaps you are. But if your organizational fitness and health is not what it should be, don't put the clothes back on until you like what you see.

36

MOTIVATED TO GET MOTIVATED!

If you look online or visit a bookstore, you will find an incredible selection of motivational books and resources. From self-help to employee motivation, the experts share their secrets of helping you and others move in a new direction with enthusiasm. If you and your staff are living and working with passion, great things can and often do happen. The trick is keeping a sustained fire burning in the belly.

If you are spending an inordinate amount of time attempting to motivate yourself or others, you might want to consider some of the following:

Figure It Out: Know the what, where, when, why and how of your plans for your career. It's tough to be motivated in a job that you don't like or that is not a fit. Some people never "get motivated to get motivated" about what they want to do when they grow up. When you just go through the motions at work, you end up going nowhere.

It's Not the Carrot or the Stick: These approaches might work on your pets, but rarely have long-term positive effects on human beings. These motivational techniques can modify short-term behavior but do not provide the kind of long-term satisfaction people get from a job they love. Carrots are simply icing on the cake for top performers and are appreciated as short-term recognition of excellent performance. Sticks are simply a reflection of failed working relationships, though unfortunately necessary in this litigious world.

Get It Right: It is critical that organizations take the time to clearly define their organizational structure, jobs and performance expectations. Otherwise it is nearly impossible to hire the most motivated people.

Hire Higher: From the person who sweeps the floor to the CEO, hire individuals who have a passion and interest in performing the required job responsibilities and duties. Use selection tools that increase the probability that your organization will hire the right individuals for open positions. When the correct alignment between job opening and candidate occurs, magic can happen in your workplace. You will be able to say goodbye to traditional supervision techniques and say hello to an approach that gives top performers the tools they need to succeed and then stay out of their way. Supported, passionate and skilled employees are the ones most likely to help your organization succeed.

Get Off the Train: Traditional corporate training will not fix bad attitudes, nor will it give people passion. Try to reserve training and education for employees eager to enhance skill sets. On the other hand, well-meaning employees who may need a spark to re-ignite their passion can benefit from motivational presentations given by other successful people.

Inspire By Example: Even the most motivated person who's in love with their job desires strong corporate leadership. They hope to find traits in that leader like a strong work ethic, honesty, job knowledge and great vision. If you are a corporate leader, one of your key jobs is to inspire by action. Words are meaningless if they're not backed up by daily personal results.

Passionate people who love their job, know their job and believe in what they are doing are more demanding of themselves than any expectations you can place on them. There may be nothing more powerful in business than attracting and retaining highly talented and motivated individuals to be on your team. The more you have, the better your chances of organizational growth and excellence. The concept works with many companies. The real question is: Why isn't every organization motivated to go this route?

37

WORK ON OUR GAMES

———————

Many years ago a story appeared in the newspaper about Michael Jordan's work ethic. Arguably one of the best, if not the best basketball players of the modern era, Jordan was renowned for his fierce competitive nature and dedication to always taking his game to the next level. He reportedly practiced harder and longer than anyone on his team, including practicing foul shots after games, long after the crowds were gone.

Pretty impressive considering he was earning millions of dollars, had reached international stardom and was in the process of leading his team to yet another championship. Why did a guy who had achieved so much still find it necessary to maintain such a rigorous practice regimen?

Many types of professionals invest time in practicing to maintain and improve their performance. Sports teams have training camps and practice sessions throughout their seasons, musicians and actors have rehearsals, pilots work on simulators and great speakers practice their presentations, voice inflections and gestures.

What about business people? How often do we practice on our employees and customers instead of practicing tough conversations and big presentations ahead of time?

For instance, there are some salespeople who are notorious for practicing on their customers. Perhaps you have encountered a few. I have witnessed horrible presentations by salespeople who plied their trade by winging it with clients. Amazingly, they still occasionally made a sale, creating further illusions that their approach to sales worked. Who knows how good some of these people could have been if they actually worked on their skill sets?

Conversely, about 25 years ago I worked for an outplacement and staffing firm. I remember walking into our CEO's office one day to find him pacing back and forth reciting what I later found out was a brief presentation he was to deliver the next day. I asked him what he was doing and he replied, "practicing." I was stunned. Here was a guy who was very successful and at the top of his game; why on earth did he need to practice? It was a defining moment for me. Working with him over the years, I saw that his incredible success was a direct result of his work ethic behind the scenes. He not only practiced presentations, but also interactions with staff, bankers and customers, preparing himself for objections and for success.

Perhaps, once in a while it may make sense to assess the following:

- Do employees practice their skill sets in your organization?
- Does your organization support training with interactive role-playing for all levels of employees?

- Does your organization employ people who love their work and have a desire to improve their skill sets?

- Does your organization promote the idea that employees should never practice on the customer?

Practice is essential for improving the odds that peak performance can be achieved and sustained when it really counts. Practice helps to reduce the probability of mistakes. Practice can make the difference between pretty good and excellent. Practice is not just for actors and athletes.

It's show time, folks. If you are in business, you and your employees play in front of a huge audience of customers, employees, service providers and the media. Practice may seem like a corny concept in business but imagine the possibilities if we were really prepared for today.

38

HOW TO FIND GREAT
EMPLOYEES

———————

CEOs and business owners often identify their number one challenge as finding and keeping qualified people for open positions. Many companies are hiring but are frustrated with the lack of candidates that meet their open jobs' requirements.

If your organization is hiring and you feel this pain, consider actions that will increase the probabilities of having great candidates attracted to your company. First, commit to hiring and keeping only top performers. This is a long-term goal and process, but the benefits of staying this course will help differentiate your organization in the eyes of top-performing people. Being known as an employer of choice among top performers in your industry and in your area will greatly enhance your ability to populate your pool of quality job applicants.

Consider the following to support your strategy:

Get Your Act Together: Is your organization a great place to work for highly skilled top performers? Make a thorough examination of your physical working conditions, compensation and benefits, workplace policies, community involvement, performance management and recognition programs. Does your organization have the right leadership in place to support the needs and interests of top-performing employees? Top performers do not last long at traditionally run, top-down managed organizations. They expect challenging jobs and workplaces that are proactive, creative, high-energy and collaborative. Plus they expect to be highly rewarded for their work and permitted to enjoy a wonderful balance with their lives outside the workplace.

Come Find Me: Organizations that successfully recruit highly qualified candidates are utilizing non-traditional strategies. Rather than just relying on placing recruitment advertisements in media outlets and on job boards, they are utilizing their professional networks, social media outlets, trade shows, professional societies and lucrative referral bonuses to employees and vendors. In addition, some companies are dedicating significant resources to industry research, identifying the top performers in their industry and then directly recruiting these individuals.

Make It a Science: If your organization hires people based on personality alone, consider adding some muscle to your program by establishing success profiles for each of your organization's jobs. These profiles, often developed in concert with a trained management psychologist, become excellent predictors of future performance and considerably aid in the selection process of job candidates. In addition, take a hard look at all of the selection tools to ensure your team is utilizing a well-thought-out approach to identifying best-fit candidates.

Managers Re-defined: Companies that are focused on top-performer recruitment and retention are re-aligning managers' jobs to those of talent managers. Managers are expected to be part of the solution of finding and keeping great people, rather than assuming the traditional role of relying solely on the human resources department. This has required managers to acquire new skill sets in networking, interviewing, research and involvement in professional societies and associations.

We Are Really Cool: Being a great workplace for top performers should not be a secret. Considerable effort and resources should be devoted to promoting your organization as a workplace that is ideal for top-performing employees. Promotions can occur through your website, social media, marketing brochures, radio, print, trade shows, displays in your reception area and, of course, through word of mouth by your employees.

If you believe that above-average performers drive your business success, then it follows that increasing their numbers in your organization is the key to producing dramatic results. Ensure that all of your employees know that you're raising the bar and that the expectation is to perform at high sustained levels. This gives quick notice to non-performers that it's time to get on or off the train. The market conditions are extraordinarily favorable now, ripe with outstanding talent. Seize the opportunity to increase the number of top performers within your company.

Who wouldn't want their organization to be filled with top performers? Top people create, innovate, provide exceptional customer service and consistently deliver more than expected and promised. In times of adversity, top performers are the ones you want on your team, and in good times you want them leading the charge. Traditional recruiting and retention practices are no longer an option. Change is a business necessity. If you are concerned about how your staff will react to radical and positive workplace change, just remember that the only individuals who will dislike these changes will be your poor performers.

Remember that differentiating your organization as a bona fide great workplace for top performers may not solve the national skills shortage, but it may solve it for your company.

39

LEADERS RE-DEFINED

There may never be a more critical time for businesses to attract, retain and motivate the next generation of workers. This will be a game changer in terms of organizational competitiveness. Talent rules, and top talent provides uncommon performance that drives organizational success. The bottom line is that the business world is changing daily, and how we lead and manage through that change will drive future company performance.

It is not hard to find a number of credible surveys about top performers and what they seek at their workplaces. These surveys provide insight on what these high-achievers expect from their jobs, their organizations and their leaders. They are re-defining the traditional views and beliefs of company leadership and leaders. Organizations that listen to and understand their top performers are ensuring they have the right type of people to lead their companies going forward.

Here are some of the key characteristics that are desired in today's corporate leadership by top performers:

Ethical: First and foremost, employees are looking to leaders to be honest and credible. With corruption widely publicized and prevalent in government and business, ethics are essential to companies wishing to sustain success.

Selfless: Leaders that genuinely prioritize others ahead of themselves gain instant respect and admiration from their peers and their workforce.

Innovative: Corporate leaders are expected to be innovative, creative and willing to try new ideas.

Listener: The days of pontificating are over. The guideline of listening 80 percent of the time and talking 20 percent of the time is becoming the rule.

Work Ethic: Nothing provides leadership by example more than demonstrating hard work and producing great results. That doesn't necessarily mean working long hours, just smart hours.

Know, Believe and Love: Leaders know what they are doing, believe in what they are doing and love what they are doing.

Winners' Circle: Great leaders associate with other great leaders and top performers.

Define Success: Leaders have a great sense of what success means in their personal and work lives.

Fit as a Fiddle: More and more corporate leaders are recognizing the importance of wellness for themselves and their workforce.

Always Happy, Never Satisfied: This philosophy sets a tone and an example for others to appreciate accomplishments but recognize the limitless possibilities for improvement.

Great Followers: If you want to lead, hire great followers.

Much of what was taught years ago about the carrot-and-stick approach to traditional management does not work anymore, particularly with your best employees. For some people at the top of their organizations, this is a tough pill to swallow. Changing their ways is difficult. Yet great leadership accompanied with great employees is the new formula for corporate and career success.

40

ROW, ROW, ROW YOUR BOAT

———————

There is a cartoon depicting two Vikings at the stern of their boat looking out to sea. Behind them are their oarsmen paddling in opposite directions from one another, with the boat traveling in circles. The caption under the cartoon reads, "We work these guys so hard, how come we never seem to get anywhere?"

Perhaps it would benefit our Viking friends if they turned around once in a while to make sure that all of their workers were coordinating their efforts.

Imagine a whole fleet of ships navigated by captains who never look back to see if their crews were working together and following orders. You might have some ships going in circles, others going forward but in the wrong direction and a few actually staying on course in spite of themselves.

What a difference it might make if the captains engaged their crews and worked with them. Not only would the ships go faster, but they'd be more efficient in route to their destinations. Morale would probably be pretty good and the possibility of a mutiny greatly diminished.

Ever feel like your organization could be the Viking ship portrayed in the cartoon described above? Are all your employees and management team rowing together? Are you keeping the boat on course?

Consider your organizational "treasure map" — your strategic plan and business goals.

A great strategy or business plan is not enough for some organizations to keep them from going in circles. Great organizations develop by having a clear map — knowing their destination, understanding their competitors, respecting the business landscape, employing the right "oarsmen" and providing the right directions and tools to perform their tasks at an extraordinary level. Yet all of these key elements are meaningless unless there is effective communication within the organization.

I know you have heard this before — communicate, communicate, communicate! But a lack of communication remains at the core of many organizational problems and frequently inhibits companies from reaching their destinations ahead of other "ships." It's easy to get so caught up in our daily routines and tasks that effective communication becomes difficult. We are so busy trying to steer the boat that sometimes we forget to work with the people moving the oars.

Here are a few ideas that might help your organization keep on track and get the team rowing together:

- Share financial information about the company on a regular basis.

- Share information about new initiatives, corporate goal

attainment and community involvement to all employees, their spouses and significant others.

- Have employees at all levels participate in the strategic and business planning process.

- Allow employees to create and modify their job descriptions.

- Provide a meaningful employee handbook that clearly highlights programs, policies and benefits.

- Ensure that all staff members understand the organization's compensation and reward system and have input into these systems' development.

- Let employees see marketing materials and advertisements before the customers and the public.

- Invite your top human resources professionals to senior management and board meetings.

- Invite members of your senior management team to HR meetings.

- Ask for feedback all the time, and do something with the information.

- Make sure all your employees understand a new product or service before they are expected to service and sell it.

- Keep your office doors open.

- Before working with a consulting firm on strategic planning, a new logo design, new product development or organizational design, ask your employees for their ideas first.

These ideas are all pretty easy, don't cost a lot of money and should become a corporate habit. Take a step back and assess how "seaworthy" your ship is for your current voyage and future travels. Sometimes it will be smooth sailing and sometimes the water will be rough.

Let's face it: Going in circles can make you pretty dizzy. And when you stop, you can look pretty silly and sometimes sink. Maybe it's time to look back and see who is rowing and who has bailed out.

41

LEADERS THAT FOLLOW (THE YELLOW BRICK ROAD)

———

Several years ago I attended a half-day program on leadership. The sponsoring organization brought in a speaker who was billed as a national leadership guru. The place was packed and heavy with anticipation of what magical thoughts the presenter would share about leading-edge leadership theory and practice.

The program started out fine, but as the morning progressed I found myself becoming disengaged with the presentation. This "guru" was losing me quick. He was very theoretical with lots of impressive words, but his presentation lacked the backing of real experience. Turns out this guru never led anything except a classroom discussion back at his university.

Needing to reload on coffee, I exited the conference room of about 400 people, refreshed my beverage and made two calls, each lasting about three minutes. When I returned, I was amazed at the mess on the presenter's overhead slides (yes, overheads). It was a myriad of lines, arrows, circles and words — all his representations of what leadership should be in an organization.

I was stunned. I didn't know whether to laugh or cry. The presentation became worse: More lines, circles, arrows and graphs poured out at a rate of one overhead a minute. I looked around. Everyone was hurriedly writing everything down, attempting to capture the essence of the presenter's leadership model. At that moment, I thought I was either really stupid or that guy had a great scam going.

The whole experience reminded me that we have a tendency to complicate the concept of leadership. Many of the participants attending this program were probably going to attempt to translate the presenter's hieroglyphics into their workplace. What a task!

Perhaps I have a simple mind, but it seems to me this whole leadership issue is pretty basic. We all learned the keys to leadership early in life from the characters of Dorothy, the Scarecrow, the Cowardly Lion and the Tin Man played in the movie *Wizard of Oz*. They taught us that vision, courage, brains and heart are what it really takes to be a leader. These four qualities are embodied in great leaders:

- Like Dorothy, they dream, have vision and are passionate about taking their organization to another level.

- Like the Lion, they are willing to take risks and demonstrate courage, standing up for what they believe.

- Like the Tin Man, they have heart, showing sensitivity and empathy for their employees.

- And, like the Scarecrow, they possess the knowledge and skills necessary to get the job done and make good decisions.

No graphs, circles, arrows or fancy words. Just four human qualities embodied in each of us that should be put to good use. The Wizard knew it, and Dorothy figured it out: real leadership is in us all the time. We don't need magic slippers like titles and corner offices to be organizational leaders. We just need to eliminate the obstacles in our heads that prohibit us from leading by example.

Pie-in-the-sky thinking? Not really. There is an ever-growing group of organizations that support and expect leadership from all their employees. These are the organizations that are growing quickly and have a reputation as great workplaces. They get it and compete effectively locally, nationally and in some cases globally.

True leadership is not as complicated as some would want you to think. So throw all the fancy diagrams and verbiage out. Leadership requires less talk and more action. Consider using the courage, heart, brains and vision already inside of you at work. Leadership is contagious; start using yours and infect someone today.

42

THANKS, BOSS!

———————

Many business leaders would agree that they would not be where they are today if everything had come easy in their careers. Most CEOs I know experienced the school of hard knocks, enduring plenty of failures, learning from mistakes and persevering even in the toughest times. As weird as it may sound, these leaders are thankful that nothing was handed to them on a silver platter. In this world of entitlement, company leaders still know and recognize that their organizations earn credibility, respect and success over time through hard work, planning and execution. Once in a while, a little luck and good timing help too.

There has been plenty of negative publicity around corporate greed and corruption over the past several decades, most of it well-deserved. Yet, there are still plenty of great company leaders out there, and we should be thankful to the good ones for:

Creating Jobs: There are still plenty of organizations growing and hiring. Behind most of these companies are a strong leadership team and CEO.

Leading by Example: Top leaders show the way and set the organizational tone.

Hiring Great Followers: They understand that hiring and keeping top performers is the key to organizational survival, innovation, growth and success.

Knowing Right From Wrong: I believe that a majority of company leaders are ethical and do the right thing. We most often hear about the bad ones, which can create an unfair stereotype of all CEOs.

Investing In Their Organizations: Whether it's employee training or new equipment, top leaders understand the value of consistently investing in their people and their business regardless of economic conditions.

Taking Risks: In a world where economics can be driven by fear and greed instead of supply and demand, great leaders stick their necks out, take chances, innovate and encourage their employees to do the same.

Giving Back to the Community: Business leaders play a big role ensuring that the community is financially supported and their employees have time to volunteer.

There are many reasons to thank good bosses in these turbulent times. If you have a great CEO or boss, let them know. It does not have to be a secret, nor does it have to be seen as political maneuvering.

Just like everyone else in the organization, bosses need and appreciate feedback, good or bad. Don't forget that your boss is a human being with feelings just like you. So next time you catch your boss doing something great, make sure you tell that person it is appreciated. You will make their day.

43

ROCK, PAPER, SCISSORS

We had a saying at a company where I once worked: "Time kills all deals." It's perhaps a blunt way of expressing how slow decision-making can hurt a business opportunity. Larger organizations seem to have a reputation of making decisions at a snail's pace, but experience dictates that organizations of any size can be stricken with this disease.

Thanks to technology, timely information is more accessible than it has ever been in history. Businesses have the information they need to make quick decisions with the assurance that the information is accurate. Decision-makers are also more accessible than ever. Round-the-clock operations have become the benchmark of availability; anything less is considered the dark ages. People are really wired these days (not just from coffee) and communicate and transmit information at lightning speed.

You would think that the tools and information available today would lead corporate decision-makers to move quickly, efficiently and remarkably accurately. Yet there are still many organizations that have a difficult time even deciding what food should be in the company vending machines.

An interesting and useful exercise is to flow-chart how decisions are made within an organization. The results might be surprising to you and your team. Take your recruiting process for example: How long does it take a qualified candidate to receive an offer from your organization, from the beginning of the recruiting process to the end? Is it a few weeks or a few months? How many good candidates have you lost because of a slow recruiting and approval process?

Considering that top talent is hard to find these days, organizations can ill-afford a recruitment and selection program that lasts more than a week or so; a slow bureaucratic process sends a message to candidates that your organization might be filled with red tape. So if molasses is faster than your decisions about candidates, don't be surprised if you have a tough time finding and keeping good people.

When I was growing up, the kids in my neighborhood had an effective decision-making tool. We played the game Rock-Paper-Scissors. Whenever there was a dispute on whether to play hide-and-seek or baseball, we would settle it with a round of Rock-Paper-Scissors. Like a scene from the stand-off at the O.K. Corral, two kids would oppose each other, right hand behind their back and on the count of three, bring their hand around formed as either a rock (a clenched fist), scissors (index and middle finger spread apart forming scissors) or paper (fingers extended and together with palm side down facing the ground). As you probably know, rocks break scissors, scissors cut paper, and paper covers rocks. This process was repeated until one of the kids won two out of three rounds. It was a pretty simple decision-making process, and it worked.

What was most interesting, was that the outcome of the Rock-Paper-Scissors exercise was final. No disputes. There was a code among us that the Rock-Paper-Scissors approach was the fairest way to make a decision and it was one that we would all live by. It certainly made our summers more fun; instead of sitting around arguing about what we would do, we made decisions and got on with being kids. What a concept!

Wouldn't it be interesting to spend a business day making decisions between two viable alternatives using the Rock-Paper-Scissors approach? Next time someone in your organization suggests a committee or task force to make an easy decision, suggest an alternate approach. Challenge them to the time-tested Rock-Paper-Scissors solution. What have you got to lose except wasted time?

44

THE WORST KIND OF TURNOVER

From creative compensation and flexible work schedules to allowing pets in the workplace, organizations are trying just about everything to attract and keep good people. There is no question that the "war for talent" among organizations, combined with a skills shortage, has created unique employment market conditions.

The scary part is that some organizations, desperate for workers, are sacrificing employee performance standards and short-cutting fundamental recruiting and selection practices. One CEO recently told me that he would hire any warm body he could find, just to keep his machines running. To further complicate his staffing problem, turnover in his company was approaching 50 percent. Yikes!

Look, people are attracted to, and stay with, organizations for a variety of reasons. The challenge today is developing a work environment that separates your organization from the pack. A commonly used term today is becoming an "employer of choice." Like selling time in a bottle, this magical mix of human resources and workplace practices is testing even the best of today's companies.

One day we will look back on this era and see that some wonderful things happened to organizations as a result of the skilled labor shortage. Businesses have become more innovative with their compensation, benefits and work-family balance programs. In addition, they have refined their training, recruitment and selection techniques and have rediscovered the human resources department. The beneficiary of these changes is the employee.

The competition is heating up trying to find and hire talented people. Consider top people analogous to free agents in professional sports. They know they are good and that they can make more money with a job move.

This is no longer a buyer's market for top people. If you identify a great candidate for your organization, ensure that you move the process along. Have a terrific on-boarding process and continue to develop an excellent work environment. Remember that time kills all deals, and if you take more than ten business days to secure a top candidate you significantly increase the risk of losing them to another company. Free agents in demand do not need to wait for you.

Today, if you really want to become an employer of choice, you had better develop a reputation for attracting and keeping great performers. Easier said than done, but not impossible. Great workplaces have developed extraordinary programs over the years that focus on creating work environments that support individual and team successes. People feel recognized, rewarded, and appreciated in these organizations. They have latitude to grow, can benefit from exceptional leaders, and are expected to perform at very high levels.

The alternative is not a rosy picture. Organizations that are not stepping up to the plate and making concerted efforts toward developing superior work environments (with all the extras), will continue to lose their competitive position in the marketplace. Perhaps they will continue to survive, but traditional practices for attracting, retaining, and rewarding employees will still produce a traditional bell-shaped curve of performance. Chances are, great performers will leave for greener pastures while the mediocre performers remain. This dynamic results in the worst kind of turnover an organization can experience – allowing poor and mediocre performers an opportunity to "quit and stay." In these organizations, "warm bodies" are the upgrade.

45

WHEN NOBODY IS WATCHING

———

"Do the right thing when nobody's watching." This quote rings so true, particularly in a work setting. Ironically, how people are judged at work and rewarded is all about what is seen rather than unseen. That's too bad, because what really dictates whether people are truly engaged with their work and your company is what they do when nobody is around to witness their performance.

Here are some questions that might provide some insight on the level of your and other employees' engagement in your organization:

- Do you or other people act or work differently when the boss is around?

- Do you or other employees clean up the kitchen, restrooms and general work areas when no one else is around, even if you did not make the mess?

- Are you or your co-workers playing politics at work and sucking up to the boss in the hopes of career or pay advancement?

- Do you or other employees use personal social media during work time when no one is looking?

- Do you or your co-workers perform work that would help out the company even if no one notices or there is no direct reward or recognition?

Fully engaged employees are ones who love what they are doing, know what they are doing and believe in what they are doing. They do so without regard to witnesses or close supervision.

Yet in this day and age of personal videos, selfies and social media there seems to be an unquenchable thirst for many people to have others witnessing their lives. Personal needs for affirmation by millions of people are being fulfilled through personal media supported through advanced technology. With so many people seeking daily virtual pats on the back, one might wonder if anyone does anything worthwhile anymore when no one is watching.

Most business cultures, workplace policies, performance measures and compensation systems are designed to reward observable behavior. Recognition in and outside of work typically comes from those actions that are witnessed, approved and encouraged. So who cares what anyone does when no one is watching? Perhaps we all should. Because, when you get down to it, the greatest judge of our character is staring at us in the mirror.

What I have observed in my business career is that most people want to be happy both at and outside of work. The research is clear that job satisfaction and job happiness are not necessarily aligned with money, good performance reviews or promotions. These are all important reflections of a job well done, but sustained happiness on the job comes from within. You achieve it when you are at the right place, doing the right job and feel like you are making a difference. You enjoy your co-workers, love the work environment and believe in the company's purpose or mission. When that happens, you do not need your actions to be witnessed to work hard and do the right thing.

And doing the right thing at work when nobody's watching sometimes is the difference between being a person of character or being considered a "character" by your boss and co-workers.

46

ALL BOXED IN

One of the traditional sayings in business is to "think outside the box." It is a request by some organizational leaders to rally their team to think differently and creatively. The box is a figurative concept, representing traditional, one-dimensional thinking. To think outside the box is challenging for many employees. They have spent their work lives comfortably inside the box. It's how they have been rewarded and it has kept them from making waves at work.

Interestingly enough, the box starts getting constructed in our childhood. Our imaginations become impeded by reality and the constant urgings by parents and teachers to grow up, conform and fit in. Sadly, creativity gets replaced with being graded on how well we color inside the lines.

In our youth and as adults, creativity and innovative thinking have no place in the box. Believe it or not, there are employers who actually like having their employees boxed in. It's pretty scary

---

that this thinking still exists. And where it does, companies are dying a slow or quick death. In these companies, the following statements are more the norm than the exception:

- You're lucky to even have a job."

- "It's work; it's not supposed to be fun."

- "I don't pay you to think."

- "Your job is what I say it is."

- "This is the way we've always done things."

Then there are other companies that recognize that their staff's thinking and approach to problem solving has become stagnant and ineffective. These organizations sometimes make desperate attempts to address the situation and retain "creativity consultants" to shake up their employees. Unfortunately, this may be money poorly spent, treating symptoms rather than the cause — a workplace environment that simply does not support innovative thinking. Long after the creativity consultants leave, the boxes of traditional thinking remain, with employees tightly packed into them.

You do not need to hire high-priced consultants to help with creative thinking at your workplace. If you are looking to break down boxes and workplace barriers to innovative thinking, consider some of the following:

Let Employees "Scrape Their Knees" Once in a While: Allow your team to take risks and try new ideas. Reward employees for trying something different. Consider implementing a "failure rewards" program instead of only focusing on workplace successes. Often rewarding the process versus the outcome is more meaningful and sends a clear message that trial-and-error and out-of-the-box thinking is desired and supported.

Eliminate Corporate Barriers: Archaic employment policies, demeaning rules and layers of bureaucracy simply make the box stronger, to the point where people are afraid to venture outside its walls.

Add Color: Take a trip to the local paint store and pick out some vibrant colors for your office. Better yet, ask your employees about your office décor, wall colors and carpeting. I'll bet you will get some great feedback on how to create a worker-friendly and stimulating environment.

Dress for Productivity: Consider incorporating a business casual dress code at least once a week if not daily. Remember, most kids hate to dress up, and adults are just grown-up kids.

Talk to Me! Talk with your team to find out their ideas on how you and your leadership team can support innovation, trial-and-error and creative thought. They will appreciate being asked, and you will get some great advice.

No More Five-day Workweek: If you ask most top-performing employees, they will tell you that the traditional five-day workweek with eight-hour days is an archaic concept. They love flexible schedules and hours with a focus on productivity and results rather than watching the clock.

Women (Should) Rule: Sorry guys, but our track record in business and government is not impressive. If you still have a bunch of men running the place, it may be time to reassess your approach on who is helping you run your business. Diversifying your leadership team leads to diversified and creative thinking. If you have a glass ceiling, the best thing you can do for your business is smash it to pieces.

When you are developing and maintaining a workplace that supports creative thinking, some may consider your ideas crazy. Guess what? Crazy ideas work really well these days. Your peers may laugh at your ideas. If they do, that is typically a good sign that you are on to something great. Most likely, those ideas are the ones that could support your continued business success and even change an industry.

If you still have a box to think outside of, rip it down, toss it aside and expand your mind. Be open to new possibilities and set a course that is uncharted. It's a heck of a lot more fun than spending the rest of your career and life walled off from life's possibilities.

47

KNOW, BELIEVE AND LOVE

———————

In 2005, Steve Jobs provided a memorable commencement speech at Stanford University. Once in a while I view the speech on YouTube, as it continues to provide perspective. Here is an excerpt from that speech:

"When I was 17, I read a quote that went something like: 'If you live each day as if it was your last, someday you'll most certainly be right.' It made an impression on me, and since then, for the past 33 years, I have looked in the mirror every morning and asked myself: "If today were the last day of my life, would I want to do what I am about to do today?" And whenever the answer has been 'no' for too many days in a row, I know I need to change something.

"Remembering that I'll be dead soon is the most important tool I've ever encountered to help me make the big choices in life. Because almost everything — all external expectations, all pride, all fear of embarrassment or failure — these things just fall away in the face of death, leaving only what is truly important.

Remembering that you are going to die is the best way I know to avoid the trap of thinking you have something to lose. You are already naked. There is no reason not to follow your heart.

"No one wants to die. Even people who want to go to heaven don't want to die to get there. And yet death is the destination we all share. No one has ever escaped it. And that is as it should be, because death is very likely the single best invention of life. It is life's change agent. It clears out the old to make way for the new. Right now the new is you, but someday not too long from now, you will gradually become the old and be cleared away. Sorry to be so dramatic, but it is quite true.

"Your time is limited, so don't waste it living someone else's life. Don't be trapped by dogma, which is living with the results of other people's thinking. Don't let the noise of others' opinions drown out your own inner voice. And most important, have the courage to follow your heart and intuition. They somehow already know what you truly want to become. Everything else is secondary."

This message from Mr. Jobs is quite clear: Do what you love and live life to the fullest. In my work life, I have seen way too many people unhappy with their careers and feeling like they are in dead-end jobs. I have never figured out why someone would stay in a job they hate. These folks seem to be going through the motions and then one day look up and realize that they have not gone anywhere with their careers.

I believe that there are three essential ingredients to job and career happiness: Love what you are doing, believe in what you are doing and know what you are doing. It's a pretty simple formula. When one of these is missing, it's probably time to either figure out a way to enhance your current job or move on to another one, perhaps in another organization.

One of the first signs that work may be going a bit sour is when you start living for the weekends. If this is a pretty steady occurrence, then it may be time to examine your level of job satisfaction during the regular workweek. It's not much fun enjoying only two out of every seven days.

If you are in a challenging work situation and not loving, knowing and believing in what you are doing, consider taking some action. Do the research and think through new and better opportunities that will significantly increase your happiness about what you do for a living. It really is not too late.

48

IS THIS THE YEAR YOU HAVE ARBEJDSGLÆDE?

Chances are that you think I botched the title of this chapter. Not at all. Actually, the last word in the chapter title is the Danish word for "happiness at work." There is no English one-word equivalent, which is not surprising given our traditional views that happiness at work occurs because of money, promotions or other factors reinforced in our work cultures.

If you research some of the workplace statistics of Scandinavian companies you find that their turnover, retention of top talent, productivity and financial results are light years ahead of workplaces in other industrialized countries. They prioritize Arbejdsglæde and recognize that if achieved, outstanding individual and corporate performance follows. The concept is incredibly simple and common sense. I believe the time has come for American businesses to wake up and start copying the

Arbejdsglæde model. And for traditional managers who think this is pie-in-the-sky stuff, good luck attracting and retaining top talent over the next five to ten years! If you really want a competitive edge for attracting, retaining and engaging great talent, Arbejdsglæde is the answer. For some companies this will require huge cultural changes, but the payoff will be dramatic.

So if you'd like to achieve Arbejdsglæde, consider some of the following tips:

Find a Great Boss: A huge part of the equation of being happy at work is working with and for someone whom you respect and admire. Bad bosses are bad for you and for everyone else. There should be no tolerance for jerk bosses in business today.

KBL: As mentioned in the previous chapter, if you do not have a job in which you know, believe and love what you are doing, it's time to move on. Find a great job that meets all three of these criteria and Arbejdsglæde will be yours.

Get Fit: This is not just about losing weight. Make a commitment that you are once and for all going to get physically fit. Getting there can be life-changing and life-saving. Your productivity will soar, your waistline will shrink and you will be happier.

Here are just a few suggestions to help you and your staff reach this lofty but very reachable goal: Ask your event and meeting planners to replace donuts, muffins and bagels at all meetings and events with healthier options. Have HR set up incentives for weight loss, enhanced fitness levels and smoking cessation. If you don't have a wellness program, have someone on your team work with an outside group to create one.

Spend More Time With Family: This one can be one of the toughest to implement considering that many traditionally run businesses have restrictive workplace policies and practices. If you're the boss, let's start with you. Time to do something radical. In the next day or so, tell everyone that you expect them to be home for dinner with their family, whenever possible, for the rest of the year. That means you, too. No work on the weekends either. If your response is that this cannot be done, then perhaps you should look at your organization's structure and the individuals you have on staff.

Try This New Habit: Consider a random act of kindness toward one or two of your co-workers or people who report to you. You will make a difference in their day and yours.

Arbejdsglæde is not a crazy concept. It works. Prioritize it in your organization, and the results will be impressive. It's pretty normal to feel guilty or weird about being happy at work, but you will get accustomed to the feeling. It is re-defining career success for many. Perhaps one day, the English language will welcome Arbejdsglæde as a word and it will become one used to characterize American business. I can only hope.

49

THE GRADUATE

—————

Whenever late spring rolls around, I always get the chance to heartily congratulate parents who are watching their high school, vocational school or college student prepare to graduate. If that's you, then great job! Now share the rest of this chapter with your soon-to-be graduate.

You will soon be graduating! Hopefully you are about to complete a wonderful experience and are getting ready to enter post-high school education or the "real world" of work. In either case, here are a few pointers about the business world and people. I wish someone had told me some of these things when I graduated from high school and college. I would have avoided a lot of bumps along the way.

Define Success: Your definition of success will be a critical guiding principle on which you base many decisions. I have met many people in my 40-plus-year career who measure success by money, title, car, neighborhood or power. If you do, you might find that you end up leading a rather empty life. As you think about your definition of success, consider the importance of friends, spouse, children, family, ethics and community service in your equation. The meaning of success may change a bit as you age, and perhaps you will find that climbing the corporate ladder is a poor second to leading a good life.

Don't Grow Up: You will find that most successful businesses — the kind you want to work for — reward creativity, innovation and risk-taking. These are attributes we all possess as children. Unfortunately, in some businesses, procedures, reward systems and promotions are based on employees following the rules, playing corporate politics and being risk-averse. These types of companies kill the kid in people, and then management wonders why their employees don't innovate or take risks. Keep being a kid at heart; you will be more successful along the way and have a heck of a lot more fun.

Interviewing 101: The stories we hear from employers about interviews with recent graduates are incredible — applicants' texting during interviews, little or no eye contact in conversation and grammatical errors on resumes. Corporate recruiters are in disbelief that applicants are coming in so ill-prepared for such an important part of the job search process. The message is clear from employers: students should take a course on how to interview and then practice, practice, practice.

It's Called Work: In addition to employers, teachers provide us feedback that too many students are just not willing to work hard at their studies or are not goal-oriented. Ask any successful person and they will say that there is no substitute for hard work. They will also tell you that employees need to show up every day (sometimes early) and occasionally work late. The bottom line is that employers expect you to put in a full day and be incredibly productive. You slack off, you lose. Period.

No Clue: Employers are telling me that candidates who are recent graduates have very little knowledge about world events, the economy and local news. Employers expect employees to understand issues outside of the workplace that affect business. It's important to have well-rounded knowledge that goes beyond social media, which offers information that has little application in the real world.

Experience Counts: Employers love seeing that students applying for jobs have experience working. For college graduates, that means employers are looking for work experiences through previous internships, preferably in job-related industries. Also, past employer references are impressive to employers. Decent grades are no longer the pathway to a great job. Real work experience, plus excellent grades and community service rank very high with many employers these days.

Master Communication: It is critical that you can read, write and publicly present well. These skill sets are essential to getting along with others, selling your ideas, resolving conflict and contributing to your company. In addition, your ability to converse one-on-one or with groups will be an essential factor in your career success. If texting has diluted your interpersonal skill sets, you'd better brush up on how to engage in conversation without the keypad. One more tip: Don't forget to turn off your cell phone in interviews, meetings, presentations and your boss' office.

Keep Learning: Your graduation simply marks the end of one educational era. In reality, you are just beginning the learning process, as you have about another 40 years of education. Read all you can, including general literature and career-related information. Ask plenty of questions and don't be afraid to continually challenge yourself with new ideas, skill sets and technology.

Flame On: Probably the most important part of your career is to be doing something that you enjoy. Living for the weekend is a horrible way to live. If you are not enjoying work most days, you are probably in the wrong profession or company. If this happens to you during your working career, take action and move on. Do not stay in a dead-end profession or job because you have a mortgage to pay.

Fail: It's OK to fail once in a while. That simply means you are trying something new. Great organizations recognize this and support employees who at least try to do something different, creative and innovative. Remember, the people they write about in history books had many more failures than successes. So during your career, make history and make a difference.

Join the Winners' Circle: If you plan to work for others, find a great workplace. Do the research and identify companies that are known for treating their employees well, supporting career growth, are ethical and have a history of delivering high-quality products or services. In addition, surround yourself with other high achievers, both at work and outside of work.

Avoid Jerks: There are plenty of great managers out there. Find them, work for them and learn from them. Unfortunately there are a few bad apples. If you find one, get out fast. They can and will make your life miserable. Life is too short to put up with their nonsense.

Balancing Act: I wish you great balance between work, play, friends and family. Work is not everything, and I hope it does not become that for you. If you can figure out a way to manage your life holistically, you will find that your time at work is more fun and satisfying.

Lead: There is a huge leadership void in our country and in business today. Because of this void, you and your generation have a tremendous opportunity to make a big difference. Take the lead on ethical business operations, developing and maintaining great workplaces, taking risks and giving back to the community.

It's been more than 40 years since I graduated from college. The time went by in a blink of an eye, and it will for you too. If you know, believe and love what you're doing, you will find unlimited career success rather than just getting a job. There is a huge difference, you'll see.

50

TIME IN A BOTTLE

———

It seems like we're all working more hours these days. Many of the recent surveys about the American worker suggest that this perception may be true. When you add in hours committed to family, home and community, there seems to be no time left for oneself.

"I never seem to be able to get ahead. I feel like I have lost control over my life," exclaimed a friend of mine. "Life seems so complicated anymore, plus they are really putting the pressure on us at work. I wish I could have an extra day each week just to get my act together. If they sold time in a bottle, I would pay a million dollars for it!"

Unfortunately for my friend, time has not yet been bottled, but there are a variety of ways to squeeze more time out of a day, week and year with just a few fairly easy steps. Some of these may ring a bell if you've attended a time management course, while others may provide new insights on managing *Father Time*:

———

Don't Hit the Snooze Button: Try getting out of bed 30 minutes earlier than normal. If you get up at 6:00 a.m. on workdays, try getting up at 5:30 a.m. Better yet, forget sleeping in on the weekends and wake up at the same time you would on weekdays. Just counting weekdays, you just earned yourself an extra two-and-a-half hours each week, or more than two weeks in a year.

Make a Plan: Try to plan every workday. If you plan, the odds of controlling your day are in your favor. Without a well-thought-out plan, you are subject to having the day's occurrences control you. It's the difference between being proactive and efficient versus reactive and inefficient. It's tough to quantify the actual time saved for this practice, but the reduced stress levels and increased efficiencies will make you wonder how you ever managed your work-life otherwise.

Block Time: An important part of planning a workday is ensuring that you block time out each day for critical telephone calls or projects in progress. Time-blocking will allow you to be much more efficient with your time and allow you to complete projects, calls or other tasks on or ahead of schedule.

Turn Off the TV: Add up the number of hours you watch television each week. You may be amazed at how much of your free time is spent as a couch potato. Perhaps there are a few shows you can live without. Not only will you save some big-time hours each week by significantly reducing your TV time, but you may find that you become more active, read more and have more conversations with people you care about. Try it for one week. If it doesn't work, what did you really miss?

Cut Meeting Time: Reduce the number and lengths of workday meetings. There seems to be an unspoken rule that all work meetings should last at least one hour. Instead of one-hour meetings, try 45- or 35-minute meetings. Work at cutting corporate bureaucracy, committees and taskforces, which can slow decision-making and rob you of valuable time.

Creating more time in your day is a challenge, but one worth working toward. We have one shot on this good earth, so we should make the best of our time. If you are letting the precious gift of time pass you by, maybe it's time you started to bottle some of your own.

51

GROUNDHOG DAY

Comedian Bill Murray starred in the lead role in the 1993 movie *Groundhog Day*. If you haven't seen the movie, here's the essence of the story: His character replays the same day over and over again. He has multiple chances to change his behavior day after day and finally does, resulting in a traditional Hollywood happy ending.

Sometimes it can feel like we are experiencing a similar Groundhog Day scenario. The headlines of the day may be different, but stories are essentially the same. Political polarization, corruption, a challenging economy, and the list goes on and on. Many people I know have turned off mainstream media because they are sick and tired of hearing about only bad news. Unfortunately, the repeated negativity and lack of real positive change have left many jaded and even apathetic.

Like the character in the movie, we have an opportunity every day to change our behavior, regardless of what is happening outside our control. Some people take advantage of these daily opportunities, and some do not. Each day is truly a gift, and it's a personal choice of whether or not to make a positive dent in a crazy world. It's easier to do nothing, complain and hope that someone else figures out a way to make this world better.

Make no mistake, even the smallest positive action results in making the world a better place. In my travels I see it with a number of great companies. I hear about the little and big changes people and organizations make to improve, to get better and to achieve more. It's cool to see and it's inspirational. If you are one of the change makers, keep it up. You are making a huge difference. If you are seeking a few ways to make a positive impact on other employees or prospective employees, consider the following:

Say Thanks! Showing appreciation to co-workers and those who report to you is a low-cost, high-yield action you can take at work. Make sure it is genuine, consistent and appropriate.

Quit Complaining: Complaining about work or your company gets you nowhere, except to a reputation as a negative person. Attitude is everything, so consider bringing a great one to work every day. If you don't like your job, try to make it great. If you have tried everything, then it is probably time to find another job. Life is too short to live for the weekends. Enjoy each day; tomorrow is not promised.

Don't Leave Anything on the Court: If you go to work every day, go to work every day. Give 100 percent effort, and the probability of great things happening for your job and your career will skyrocket. Have a goal to make your workplace better each and every day.

Take Responsibility: This is your work life so manage it well.

Take full responsibility for your actions, be accountable and, of course, honest. Your credibility at work is an essential component of your work life and career success.

Lead: You do not need a management title to lead by example. Knowing, believing and loving what you do at work sets a positive tone for everyone around you. If you do have a management title, earn it every day.

Have Fun! Nothing brightens up a workday more than smiles and laughter. Appropriate and well-timed humor helps us all face tough business challenges and rough work days. Good moods are infectious!

If you are struggling at work for whatever reason, perhaps a few of these tips will help. Challenge yourself to make some positive changes. The end result will most likely be a better work environment and a renewed energy about your job and your organization. Just remember, make today better than yesterday and then repeat that approach tomorrow. Now, that would be a great Groundhog Day!

52

COFFEE STAINS AND JET ENGINES

Several years ago, an airline CEO made quite a memorable statement. In a speech before a group of business leaders, he pointed out how customers correlate certain items with airline safety. He stated that, "coffee stains on a seat could get a passenger to wonder about the maintenance of the plane's engines." You could hear a number of people in the audience chuckle at the thought, while others raised eyebrows of fascination.

This airline CEO's point was really very simple. Customers might judge product reliability or safety based on factors apparently unrelated to the actual service or product. In his particular example, the plane's engines might be perfect, but a passenger might question the airline if it could not even maintain the cleanliness of its passengers' seats.

A few jobs ago, I worked at a healthcare facility. We

administered several patient satisfaction surveys throughout my eight-year tenure; interestingly enough, quality was often viewed by patients in terms of physicians' bed side manner, wait time for appointments, cleanliness of exam rooms, friendliness of the staff and correct invoices. Rarely was "getting better" a determinant of the perception of healthcare quality!

Now, we all know that coffee stains on a passenger seat do not affect jet engines and that patient wait time does not mend a broken arm. But there are great lessons to be learned from customers. Though you may have the best product or service around, your organization might not be paying attention to some of the other cues identified by customers that affect a buying decision.

Are current and potential customers seeing that your organization's "music matches its dance?" Think about all of the opportunities to make an excellent business impression. From your lobby and staff to the vehicles transporting your goods and services — each should match up with the wonderful images and messages in your organization's marketing literature, website and social media.

For your customers and prospective customers, take a look at wait time, telephone on-hold recordings, cleanliness of your organization's lobby and parking lot, and even your signage and business cards. Are you and your team sending consistent messages about your organization's ability to perform?

And don't forget your employees; they are your internal customers. For employees and prospective employees, are your employment policies, compensation and benefit programs, physical working conditions and management's leadership matching up with the promise to provide a great workplace?

Perhaps it's time to consider conducting ongoing customer and employee engagement surveys. You may be surprised at what really matters to your employees and customers. Sweating the small stuff and paying attention to detail can make or break decisions about customer purchases or attracting top talent.

Great customer service only happens if you are successful at finding and keeping terrific employees. In this increasingly challenging business climate, organizational success is happening to those companies who understand this relationship. So, if you have employees who are ensuring your company's "coffee stains" are cleaned up, your organization is probably flying high. If not, then your business might never really get off the ground.

53

REGISTER A COMPLAINT!

When I was a child, my mom would take me with her on a variety of errands. Food shopping was not on my top ten favorite things to do list, but my mom had a knack for making every trip fun. She routinely turned the checkout line into a game; we would try to stuff as much food as possible on that black conveyor belt to see if the cashier could keep up with us. It was a battle won weekly by the cashiers, for they were incredibly skilled and adept at their craft. In addition to being good at their job, the cashiers knew their customers, called them by name and typically wore a smile even during the busiest of times. It was not uncommon for the cashier to even remember my name from the week before. Imagine that!

Something certainly has changed with most shopping experiences since I was a kid. Unfortunately the smiling cashier from yesteryear who knew everyone's name has apparently vanished, along with great customer service. In too many stores, the cashier has become a faceless person who occasionally looks up and makes brief eye contact. The gratuitous "thank you" for shopping at their store only adds to the rather cold interaction that seems to be far too routine and accepted.

A smile or a pleasant "hello" appears to be an effort and shocks me when it occurs. In fact, words typically uttered by the cashier are often in the form of a complaint about the store management or that she or he has been working all day and needs a break. The real entertainment occurs when a three-way complaint session ensues between the neighboring cashiers. The squabbling and pettiness about their company is pitiful and inappropriate. The complaining cashiers act as though customers aren't even there.

Complaints about poor customer service from food stores to retail shops to airlines are all too common today. Consultants, trainers and authors are having a heyday with corporate America by making millions of dollars from companies trying to correct poor customer service. There is no quick fix, but perhaps the issues are not as complex as consultants would want you to believe. Here are a couple of basic concepts that might be food for thought if your organization is having issues providing great customer service:

- Customer service training makes sense for employees interested in making improvements and who care about their jobs, your company and, of course, the customer. Try to avoid providing customer service training to employees who dislike their jobs. If you do, you are only giving them some paid time away from the work they hate.

- Great customer service happens when employees know what they're doing, believe in what they are doing and love what they're doing. Focus your efforts around developing good jobs for top-performing people and "wow" customer service will happen naturally.

- Great customer service begins at the top of the organization. Management needs to lead by example by providing uncommon service and support to employees and customers.

- Ensure that all employees understand that great customer service is the expectation and not the exception. Again, these expectations are welcomed by top-performing people. Poor performers couldn't care less.

- Publicly recognize employees who provide extraordinary customer service. These can be cash or non-cash awards. In either case, those providing the great service get acknowledgement for a job well done while performance expectations are reinforced with other employees.

- Ask your staff for creative ideas on providing great customer service. Your top performers have fabulous ideas on how to impress customers. Tap into their thoughts. Not only is it cheaper than hiring a high-priced consultant, but the advice will probably be better.

Implementing these concepts can help your company differentiate itself in a competitive marketplace. There may be nothing more compelling to a customer than being wowed by your service. News travels fast, and positive word of mouth is the best form of advertising.

If you are serious about taking your organization to the next level, delivering consistently uncommon customer service is critical. If you do that, look out! You will dramatically improve the probability that your organization will capture the lion's share of your market. And maybe, just maybe that cashier I met so long ago will return.

54

RUDY'S

———

Growing up in the small town of Willowick, Ohio, there was only one place my mom and neighbors would shop for their meat and poultry — Rudy's Quality Meats. Back in the day, there was a food market called Pick-n-Pay at Shoregate Shopping Center. My mom would grocery shop there for everything except what Rudy's offered. I remember as a kid going there with my mom and being treated like royalty. When you walked in the door they even called you by name as they welcomed you into their market. I also recall that everyone behind the counter seemed happy and also worked really hard.

Grandpa Rudy Bukovec started the business nearly a century ago. It's still located on Vine Street just up the way from Lake Shore Boulevard, and not much has changed there since I was a child. Though I don't live there anymore, I still travel to Willowick to purchase meat and poultry from Rudy's after our regular grocery shopping. You are still welcomed by name, and they still work hard with a smile.

As a lifelong student of business I am fascinated with how consistently successful they are, year in and year out. With no website, no social media and very little formal advertising, Rudy's busts at the seams with customers (at least every time I'm there). There are a number of lessons to be learned from this business, which boasts four generations of family either owning or working at Rudy's:

Serve From the Heart: Anyone who shops at Rudy's on a regular basis recognizes that the people who work there have a genuine interest in helping customers. The smiles on their employees' faces come naturally because they love their work.

Appreciation and Respect: Though they have been in business for nearly a century, the owners of Rudy's continue to be grateful for new customers and never take their long-term customers for granted. Perhaps it comes from their strong family values of mutual respect for each other and for those that walk through their doors. It is pretty cool to see, and unfortunately uncommon in many other retail establishments these days.

Value: People shop there because they know the quality of the product is consistently excellent.

Retention of Top Performers: I have to imagine that their employee turnover is low, since I see the same faces year in and year out behind the counter. Make no mistake — they don't stick around because the work is easy. They define hustle, excellent service and knowing what they are doing.

Word-of-Mouth Marketing: The customer experience and quality of product has earned them such an outstanding reputation that their customers do all of their marketing for them.

I am living proof since I felt so compelled to write about this remarkable business. It is not only neighbor telling neighbor but second and third generations of long-time customers coming into their store. Again, my family is proof of that as we on our fourth generation of Rudy's shoppers.

"How's Your Mom?" When I stop in to shop, the first question they ask me is "How is your mom?" It's not "How can I help you today?" The inquiry about my mom comes from multiple employees. More impressive is that they are asking because they are interested. This type of conversation is echoed right down the counter line as long-term friendships have been built over the years, epitomizing a throwback to the great American neighborhood business. It's refreshing, uncommon and most appreciated in this crazy, complicated and high-tech world.

Many cities across the nation are fortunate to still have healthy, independent, long-time local businesses like Rudy's that run their business on the fundamentals of being successful, and still truly care about their customers.

55

ARE YOU PROFESSIONALLY FIT?

If you are attempting to get into better physical shape, you've faced the virtually unlimited number of options and approaches promising to help you accomplish this goal. Many are pretty good, but it comes down to choosing a common sense approach and sticking with it. If you have discipline and motivation, your odds of experiencing success are quite high.

Being physically fit at work also has many benefits including being more productive, able to better handle stress and fewer illnesses that lead to absenteeism. There is a tremendous amount of research on the topic, much of it pointing to the same conclusion: Job performance and physical fitness are positively correlated. Fitness experts agree that exercise, diet and proper rest all play a crucial role in getting and maintaining a physically fit body.

Workplaces have taken notice over the years of these compelling research findings. Today it seems to be an exception if a company does not have some sort of corporate health and wellness program available for its workforce. Companies that support these types of programs recognize that the benefits for employees outweigh the financial investment many times over.

In addition to your physical fitness, how much emphasis do you place on your professional fitness? Like an athlete who prepares his or her body to compete, how well have you prepared yourself to perform at your very best in the workplace and develop the experience and skill sets needed to elevate your career? If you do not have a professional fitness game plan, here are a few thoughts to consider:

Image: How we look and feel are typically how we gauge our physical fitness level. It's no different in your career. Like it or not, the first indication of your professional success is often judged by your resume, your ability to articulate your thoughts intelligently — both verbally and in writing — as well as your wardrobe, business photo, manners, overall professionalism and image. Social media also plays a role in how people might perceive your professionalism, credibility and success; what you write and the photos you publish may alter or enhance how people view you at the workplace and in your career. As an example, if you have a selfie on your LinkedIn profile that might not be flattering — perhaps one taken at midnight on New Year's Eve — consider replacing it with a photo that better represents you and your company.

Exercise: We know that exercise plays a key role in supporting health and well-being. Equally important in building your professional fitness is exercising your mind on the job with challenging work and lifelong learning opportunities. Careers are similar to marathon races: They are long, challenging and take plenty of training to compete effectively.

Rest: Many jobs are very demanding and can take a toll mentally and physically. Without time away from the job and restful sleep, getting run-down and burnt-out can significantly alter performance and job satisfaction. Taking a break isn't just time away from the office, it's quality time away from the office. Unfortunately, technology has placed many employees in a 24/7 accessibility mode, even though they are physically away from work. If possible, disconnect when the work day is done as it makes a world of difference in the short and long term.

What the Fittest Want: High achieving employees love working at companies where there is a prevalence of other top-performing people. Being around others who share your passion for job and career success makes a big difference in the quality of your life at and outside of work. It's motivational, fun and challenging.

When you look in your "career mirror" do you like what you see? If not, these are some steps you can take to improve your overall professional fitness and increase the probability that you will meet and exceed your career goals.

To achieve and maintain a high level of physical fitness takes a lot of work, sweat, dedication, discipline and motivation. It's not easy, just as it's not easy to achieve career success. If you want to end up knowing, believing and loving what you do at work it may be time to set up your professional fitness plan. When you work towards physical and professional fitness concurrently, you will find that the quality of your life at and outside of work becomes exceptional. So set up your plans and get ready to work out!

56

WHEN YOUR COMMUTE
BECOMES WORK

———————

Recently I was stopped at a red light where cars were exiting off the freeway onto the road I was driving on. It was fascinating and scary to see that the majority of drivers were making their turns while texting or looking down at their phone. I then looked to my right to see the driver next to me texting. Then I looked in my rearview mirror and the driver behind me was showcasing an apparent text to her fellow passengers while they waited for the light to change. I realized that the vehicles surrounding me were being driven by people who apparently had more important things to do than drive their cars!

Perhaps you have experienced a similar scenario. Seems like wherever I travel these days, the use of mobile devices while driving seems to be the norm versus the exception. Consider how many people during rush hour are paying more attention to an incoming message on their phone rather than the traffic in front of them!

Beyond mobile phone usage by commuters while driving their vehicles, there are a number of other potential hazards when attempting to get to work via the roadways. Here are several classifications of drivers to try to avoid who could increase the probability of a minor to fatal car accident:

Gators: These are the drivers who believe that if they nearly attach themselves to the rear end of your vehicle they will somehow get to their destination faster. This occurs even in bumper-to-bumper traffic. When I have one of these Gators behind me, I simply move over and allow them to merrily go on their way. Interestingly enough, they move up to the next car in the lane and repeat their madness. It reminds me of NASCAR drivers drafting off other cars in a race. Once in a while a Gator who has been on my tail for a minute or two, will pass me and let me know that I am No. 1 by waving to me using a particular hand gesture. This always brings a smile to my face. They must be thanking me for paying attention to the speed limit.

Makeup Artist: This person applies makeup while looking in their rearview mirror and driving at the same time. It must take years of practice to get really good at applying makeup in a vehicle moving between 60 and 80 miles per hour.

Foodie: In addition to a few sips of coffee, this commuter enjoys a bountiful meal during their drive to work. Whether it is fast food or something they prepared at home, the Foodie presumably has perfected the ability to gulp down breakfast while traveling at high speeds without a mess on their clothes or in their car.

The Talker: Easy to spot, the Talker usually has their head bent to one side, cradling their phone with their neck, and conducting a fully animated conversation. The driver's arms can be seen moving around (not on the wheel) as he or she evidently makes an important point to the person on the other end of the line. I guess this is the Talker's version of using their mobile device hands-free.

Multi-tasker: This driver combines two or more of the actions described above. I assume that the Multi-tasker is supremely confident that he or she has mastered some combination of texting, eating, talking on the phone and applying makeup while operating a motor vehicle.

Actually, none of this is funny. It is amazing given the number of distracted drivers that more accidents don't occur. Of course, the last thing anyone wants is an accident, especially one where someone gets injured. My assumption is that most people desire a job where the work is challenging. Hopefully we are not at a time in our lives when achieving a safe commute has become the biggest challenge of our workday.

57

OUT OF THIS WORKPLACE

I had a really crazy dream the other night. The dream started out innocently enough. I was sitting on my back deck watching the sunset. As evening approached, I gazed into the night sky and was startled by what I thought was a shooting star. It was quite beautiful and filled the night sky with brilliant light. This shooting star was certainly something special. Suddenly, it came right at our house and in a flash exploded into our backyard.

Scared to death, I approached the burning object and discovered what appeared to be an alien aircraft. In a split second, a door opened and out jumped what appeared to be a young man. He smiled, extended his hand and introduced himself as Jack. Instinctively, I reciprocated with a handshake and smile.

"Who are you?" I asked.

"I am a visitor from another planet," Jack replied.

"Why are you here?" I continued.

"Actually, I was trying to leave your planet when my ship

malfunctioned. I have been visiting Earth for about a month and was attempting to head back home," Jack said.

"Wow, this is really cool," I blurted out. "Are you friendly? What were you doing here? Why are you leaving? Are you bringing others back?" In fact, I followed those questions with about fifty more before Jack could respond.

"Slow down, earthling," he said. "I will answer your questions, but then you need to answer a few of mine. Is that a deal?"

"Of course," I replied excitedly.

"I was visiting Earth from a distant planet on a research mission," Jack said. "My species is very friendly and we have no interest in harming you or any of your kind. In fact, I doubt we will come back. Though we look human, we are not. We are fairly advanced as compared to your people."

I just sat there with my jaw in my lap as Jack went on to explain that he was simply the equivalent of an Earth college student. He was here to complete a research paper on Earth's workplaces for a course he was taking back on his planet. He thought he might fail the course, because he was leaving without answers to his research questions. I let him know that I could provide the answers he needed and then hopefully help him get on his way.

"Great, earthling!" Jack responded happily. "I appreciate your interest in helping me and if you do, I will be eternally grateful. But I am not sure you can answer these questions. I have searched for the answers, but cannot find logical explanations anywhere."

"Just try me," I said confidently.

"OK, earthling. Here we go," stated an eager Jack. He began rattling off his questions:

"Why do your managers in your planet's organizations keep doing annual performance reviews if they hate the process?"

"Why do so many earthlings go to places called 'work' unhappily everyday?"

"Why are new employees put on probation? Did they do something wrong?"

"Why are your planet's professional athletes paid and praised more than earthlings that save lives, find cures for diseases or teach your offspring?"

"Why do some organizations have candy and chips in their vending machines, but get upset about their rising health insurance costs?"

"Why do some companies provide a list of people in their bereavement leave policies that your earthling workers can mourn if someone on that list dies? Are your earthling workers not permitted to mourn others who aren't on the list?"

"Why do they call it work-life balance if your workers still spend more time at work than with their families?"

"OK, Jack, enough," I pleaded. "There is no logical explanation for any of your questions."

Jack just stared at me. He sheepishly grinned and replied, "I didn't think so."

At this point he had finished his repairs and stated that his ship was ready for a re-launch. He extended his hand and thanked me for my time and the conversation. He wished me well as he climbed back into the ship. The door closed shut and then suddenly reopened.

"Hey earthling, I forgot one more question," he said.

"What's that?" I replied.

"What's stopping you earthlings from figuring out the answers to my questions?" he mused.

With that, the cockpit door closed and in a flash his ship was off to the heavens. I remember the earth shaking terribly when he took off, which turned out to be my spouse waking me up.

"Pat, do you know you were talking in your sleep?" she asked. Upon gaining full consciousness, I quickly shared my dream with her. After hearing my story, she commented that the questions were great; perhaps every organization could use them to stimulate improvement in their workplace.

With a sigh I responded, "Yeah, only in my dreams."

Like Jack, my guess is that you have plenty of questions too. Some are head-scratchers and others just result from human nature. What I have learned is that really good organizations try to create and maintain work environments where common sense is the rule rather than the exception. They also encourage employees to raise their hands and challenge the status quo so that the workplace continues to be enhanced over time.

If you work for a company where things just do not seem right, what is stopping you from raising your hand and asking questions? You already know the answer to that question. So my question to you is, why stay?

58

THE MOST IMPORTANT QUESTION

At your next management retreat, begin by asking your leadership the following: "What is the question we need to answer most in our organization to significantly increase our odds for sustained business success?" Give your managers five minutes to write down their question and then ask them to present it and their reasons for choosing it, to the group.

The answers you receive will provide insight into your leaders' psyches, and will give you a baseline for some interesting conversations throughout the remainder of your meeting. Most managers will likely identify questions related to tactical and strategic initiatives, ranging from the basic to the sophisticated.

So, what's the answer? Sounds like a riddle, but it's pretty simple. The question that every management team should be asking themselves is: "Are we committed to attracting and retaining only top performers?" The answer is a simple "yes" or "no." An answer of "yes" shows that the organization is prepared to commit to managing their workplace differently than traditionally-run organizations.

I have run into CEOs who believe that hiring and keeping only top people is impossible and unrealistic. Truthfully, attaining that pinnacle is a bit idealistic, but trying to achieve that goal is doable. Ongoing attempts can yield dramatic, positive organizational results.

If you and your team are interested in pursuing this challenge, consider the following seven workplace attributes desired by top performers:

Flexibility: Top performers want the flexibility necessary to manage life inside and outside of the workplace. This might include flexible work schedules, liberal paid time-off policies, a non-traditional bereavement leave policy (taking as much paid time off from work to grieve for a loved one until the employee is ready to return) sabbaticals and employee benefits like convenience services.

Opportunity: Top performers want opportunities to advance within the organization and utilize their abilities to impact the company and the community. They want challenging and interesting work, as well as opportunities to be engaged in the success of the business. Examples include promotions from within, succession planning, suggestion systems, employee surveys and community service.

Recognition: Top performers want to feel appreciated. They want to be adequately compensated and rewarded for their efforts and their accomplishments. Examples include pay-for-performance programs, bonus plans, incentive pay, internal and external equity, ad-hoc cash and non-cash rewards, a well-aligned compensation philosophy and public and peer recognition programs.

Development: Top performers want opportunities to further their professional and personal development and advance their skills. They want feedback about their performance and about how they can improve. Examples include training and development programs, training needs assessments, non-traditional performance appraisals, tuition reimbursement and career coaching.

Security: Top performers want to work in a healthy and safe environment free from accidents, violence, harassment, layoffs and discrimination. Organizations that support a safe, secure and healthy workplace focus on emergency and safety training, wellness programs, workplace violence prevention, disaster recovery programs, harassment training and policies, and cultural awareness training.

Support: Top performers want benefits that help support their physical and mental health and help them address other issues in their lives outside the workplace. Examples include medical, dental and vision insurance; short-term and long-term care; adoption assistance; child care and elder care; wellness programs; and convenience services.

Talent Integrity: Top performers want to work in an environment where they can relate to, get along with and be challenged by their co-workers. They want to be surrounded by other top performers. Organizations working toward hiring and retaining top performers utilize hiring assessments, behavioral interviewing, stay interviews, exit interviews, succession planning, non-traditional recruiting methods and mentoring programs.

Hiring and keeping top people means developing and maintaining a great workplace. It takes throwing out some archaic policies and programs designed eons ago for poor-performing or problem employees. It takes some guts, and will definitely challenge the status quo.

If you want to expedite developing your workplace to attract and keep the best, there is an easy way to start. Just ask your top people how to proceed. Their responses will be the most important answers you can receive to support your organization's ongoing success.

59

RE-THINK PAID TIME OFF

───────

Many traditional paid time-off policies are based upon employee tenure. For instance, employees with one to five years of employment with a company might be eligible for two weeks of vacation per year, while those with five to ten years of employment get three weeks of paid vacation, and so on. It's also common to have a waiting period of 90 to 120 days for first-year employees to earn paid time off. There is also often a provision that all eligible employees need to use earned vacation by year-end or lose it.

Back in 1998, the company I led, instituted an unlimited paid time-off policy for all employees.I mention the year, because at that time, that type of policy was completely new in business and industry. Proudly, we were the pioneer or at least one of the first companies in the U.S. to attempt such an initiative.

Our management team never gave a second thought to implementing the program, since many of us had been subject to structured and limiting paid time-off programs for years with previous employers. At the same time, we eliminated other archaic benefits and policies that would negatively affect our ability to attract and retain talented people. The no-limit paid time-off program survived two decades and I believe is still going strong at my former company.

If your organization still has a traditionally structured paid time-off program, here are some thoughts to consider:

It's About Time: Unfortunately many organizations still embrace policies that originated in the workplace 30 to 50 years ago. Programs like structured paid time-off programs, probationary periods and restrictive bereavement leaves have certainly not changed with the times. If you are really serious about top talent populating your company, then an assessment of your workplace policies might be in order. Outdated and structured programs send a clear message to people about your culture and work environment.

Trust: The no-limit paid time-off policy always makes for good conversation. Many of my peers argue that they could never implement this type of program because employees would abuse the policy. My response is the same every time: "Why are you employing people that you do not trust?" Like many structured programs, policies and guidelines in today's workplace were created to address challenges created by the few people in companies that don't perform and cannot be trusted.

It's a shame that the rest of the well-intentioned, high-performing people in companies need to endure archaic policies because of a few rotten apples. Top performers by the very definition are people you can trust. Ask them and they will tell you that they would love less structured workplace policies that allow them flexibility, autonomy and a feeling that they are actually being treated like adults.

Focus on Job Performance: Top-performing employees are much more focused on results than ensuring they use up all their vacation days under a traditional lose-it-or-use-it paid time-off program.

Competitive Edge: If the statistics from the human resources professional organizations are accurate, most companies do not have unlimited paid time-off programs. By implementing such a program, it creates an incredible opportunity for companies to stand out from the crowd and further enhance their reputation as an employer of choice.

At the very least, consider looking at new and different approaches to paid time off and other polices that were designed long ago for a different work world. It is truly a new day in the workplace. Employee expectations and work styles have changed significantly over time, requiring organizations to take a hard look at what they are doing to attract and retain quality employees. It just might be time for traditional paid time-off polices to take a permanent vacation.

60

COMMUNITY INVOLVEMENT IS A BUSINESS WIN

———————

In 1979, I started my career in Northeast Ohio at an international CPA firm. I was fortunate to find a great job in my hometown near family and friends. One of the memories from that first job was how our firm took giving back to the community very seriously. The firm's partners expected every employee to participate in this endeavor through monetary donations. Back in the day, the level of community service was often measured against the size of the donation check written.

As evidence, my first bonus check reflected a deduction already made to the local charity, which was considered my annual fair share to the charity. For a young guy out of college, this was a bit of a shock and my first experience with a so-called "voluntary" charitable donation.

Fast forward 40 years. How area businesses support the local

RE-SHAPE RE-DEFINE RE-IMAGINE

community is a far cry from the approach used in the workplace many years ago. It's not just about the monetary donation any more. Today's workers are expecting their employers to incorporate the following relative to community involvement:

- Provide time off to allow for hands-on community-based activities. Whether it is helping out at a food bank, building a house or spending time with seniors, employees want to experience making a difference through volunteerism. The approach to time off varies by employer, ranging from time off without pay to paid month-long community service sabbaticals.

- Organize corporate-wide community service programs that provide additional opportunities for employees to learn about local needs and at the same time make a positive impact on others.

- Embrace family-first work environments where employees have the flexibility to manage family obligations, spend more time with loved ones and care for parents. Employers are responding by replacing archaic workplace policies with forward-thinking programs, which support enhanced approaches to work-life balance. And nothing builds a better community than raising good kids.

So why does any of this matter? In conversations with local business leaders, they consistently state that the No. 1 challenge they have growing their business is attracting and keeping good talent. Likewise, research shows that making a difference in the local community, through employer support, is near the top of the list for employees and job candidates.

The workplace environments that were prevalent when I started my career are just not cutting it anymore. My graduating classmates were happy to land a decent paying job with basic employee benefits. Today, talented top-performing employees seek work environments that are progressive, trusting and community-focused.

The change in employee expectations over the past four decades is significant and expected to gain momentum especially in the areas of work-life balance and community service. Making a difference in the community is not only the right thing to do, but also makes for good business when it comes to talent management. People are looking for meaning in their lives and at work. When employers step up to the plate and genuinely acknowledge and support these needs, everyone wins.

61

WHAT'S ALL THE BUZZ ABOUT?

Have you ever been in meetings at work that seemed eerily like scenes from the 1999 movie *Office Space*? The comedy hit is notable for its stereotypical portrayal of business people, bureaucracy, office politics and the overuse of business buzzwords.

Many people can identify with the business jargon used in the movie as they see it played out daily at their workplace. Typically used by managers, these buzzwords are intended to convey meaning, motivate, establish credibility, gain acceptance or to simply emphasize a point. Some managers utilize buzzwords so much, it becomes habit and an integral part of their day to day conversations. Unfortunately, buzzword use or overuse can sometimes alienate employees, customers and prospective customers.

Here is just a sampling of buzzwords or phrases used at workplaces with more being created each day:

Think outside the box, give 110%, best practices, deep dive, synergy, paradigm shift, going forward, push the envelope, Web 2.0, value-added proposition, the 80/20 rule, core competency, outplacement, let's take this off-line, take it to the next level, drop the ball, bring our 'A' game, seamless integration, scalable, at the end of the day, brings a lot of value to the table, it is what it is, let's hit the ground running, 24/7, drinking the Kool-Aid, have a seat at the table, client-centered, touch base, change agent, the bottom line, manage expectations, offline, actionable, multi-task, impactful, be proactive, ballpark figure, the 800-pound gorilla in the room, strategic, market-driven, ROI, next generation, circle back, out-of-pocket, go from good to great, get on the bus, has legs and can go really far, we don't have the bandwidth, let's get granular, rightsizing, downsizing, put a stake in the ground, gone viral, step up to the plate, don't throw out the baby with the bathwater, industry standard, world-class, raise the bar, net-net, manage expectations, user-experience, customer focused, integrated approach, perfect storm, the customer is always right, the elephant in the room, resonate, too many chefs in the kitchen, transparency, work-life balance, stakeholders, benchmark, user-focused, industry leader, thought leader, team player, company person, game changer, moving up the value chain, brainstorm, crowd-sourcing, boots on the ground, the scenery only changes for the lead dog, cast a wider net, I'm not throwing him under the bus but..., blue-sky thinking, get our ducks in a row, moving forward, boil the ocean, synergy, heavy lifting, face time, hard copy, cube farm, re-boot, desk job, kept in the loop and go after the low hanging fruit.

There are many more buzzwords and phrases that are generic or industry specific. For instance, those involved with technology have historically used language that can be challenging to understand for those of us not immersed in that profession. In addition, Information Technology professionals also have buzzwords and phrases that are now finding their way into mainstream business including; mobile first, Artificial Intelligence (AI), Blockchain, quantum computing, immersive experience, big data, Net Neutrality, Virtual Reality (VR), Chatbots and Machine Learning.

Buzzwords and business jargon will always be prevalent at work. If you do incorporate some of these terms in your conversations and/or presentations consider using them with purpose, sparingly and artfully. By doing so, your chances are pretty good that the message you are attempting to communicate will be heard. And, that will certainly be a 'win-win' for everyone concerned.

62

THE FIVE LANES ON THE ROAD TO BUSINESS SUCCESS

Conducting business day-to-day does not have to be complicated. Offer a good product or service, price it right, over-deliver to your customers, be honest and ethical. Seems pretty simple right? Unfortunately, the road to business success can be bumpy, have some detours, wicked turns and on occasion some of your competitors may not obey the 'rules of the road'. There are also temptations to take shortcuts and sometimes not follow directions.

Whether you are just beginning your journey as a business owner or have more than a few years of leadership under your belt, imagine the 'road' ahead of you to include five lanes. Navigate each lane well and ultimately they will merge together and catapult your business to destinations you and your team never thought possible.

Lane #1: Define Success – This is probably the most important lane on the road, as it is critical to define success for your business. Perhaps it is a traditional definition focused on bottom line results. Maybe your definition prioritizes your employees and their families over profits. Regardless of how you define business success, remember that your definition plays a critical role in future decision-making and provides a great benchmark along the way. Sadly, some organizations never commit to clearly defining what business success should look like for their company. These organizations 'sputter' along the road without much direction.

Lane #2: Commit to Attracting and Retaining the Best People – Once you have defined what success looks like for your business, commit to attracting and retaining only the best people who can support that definition. This lane is challenging to navigate as it requires a significant commitment to your team, versus a company that accepts less than the best. Remember that average performers will always yield average results, so hire and attempt to keep your best people.

Lane #3: Create a Great Workplace for Top Performers – Top talent expects their employers to be great places to work. Great workplaces are forward thinking and offer policies and programs that enable top performers to focus on their jobs. Top performers are supported and rewarded based on results, have flexible work options and enjoy work settings that have healthy and positive cultures. In great workplaces, top performers are free from old-style company politics, bureaucracy and traditional workplace policies like Probationary Periods and 'use it or lose it' vacation programs. If you have a traditional work setting be prepared to move over in this lane as great workplaces for top people will be passing you by at lightning speed. You simply will not have enough 'horsepower' in your business engine to keep up with these other companies.

Lane #4: Don't Worry about Competitors – In 20 years of leading my former company, I never expended unnecessary energy worrying about organizations that overlapped or copied our services. Rather, I shared with the team that our time needed to be dedicated to taking great care of customers and creating new ways to address market needs. Spending time thinking or worrying about competitors was simply wasted time. And, if your company is an industry leader, remember that other organizations who think they are competing with you are simply followers trying to catch up to your company. So, try not to spend time seeing who is driving beside you and focus on the road ahead. If you do, chances are your competitors will all end up in your 'rear-view' mirror.

Lane #5: Never Follow the Crowd – There is not much traffic in this lane because it is reserved for industry pioneers, innovators and risk takers that revel in being and thinking different. These are the admired organizations that bring new ideas and products to market. They are led by extraordinary people who dismiss the status quo and create new rules of the road for their company and their industry. They hate driving in a crowded lane and shake their heads at all the companies stuck in gridlock in other lanes that are conducting business as usual and hardly making any progress towards truly being successful.

In addition to using these five lanes, keep your eyes on the 'road', focus on driving your business to your desired destination and ensure you pause at a few rest stops along the way. Otherwise you are apt to end up at the wrong destination or be a broken down business watching other organizations fly by on their road to success.

63

WORDS REAL LEADERS SAY
MOST OFTEN

A few years ago, I had the pleasure of attending the first Holy Communion service for my niece's daughter. The Priest officiating the Mass, provided an impactful sermon to the thirty communicants. Though his comments were directed to the children, every adult in attendance benefited from the Priest's homily.

The essence of his sermon had to do with the importance of saying 'please,' thank you' and 'I'm sorry' when appropriate. Simple but vitally important practices and a good reminder for all. The delivery of the Pastor's message was riveting and certainly struck a chord.

Later that day, I re-framed his thoughts within the context of how important it is for business leaders to utilize these words. The most impressive leaders I know, would agree that please, thank you and I'm sorry might be the most important words they use in their conversations with employees, prospective employees, customers and prospective customers. Here is why:

- Employees really appreciate leaders that ask nicely. What a difference it makes on the receiving end when the boss says please when requesting tasks to be completed.

- Saying thank you costs nothing but is priceless. When shared generously and genuinely it provides employees well-deserved recognition for great effort and a job well done.

- Leaders who admit mistakes earn the respect of their employees and peers. The truth is, the boss simply can't know everything and is not always right.

Great leaders also understand how important it is to express a genuine interest in their employees' well-being and job satisfaction. This should not be confused with the casual "how are you doing" as you pass employees in the hallway at work. Leaders also ask about employees' families, which is another reflection that the boss actually cares.

Employees do listen carefully to a leader's words and how they are delivered. Actions often do speak louder than words and also support the words spoken by those in charge. That being said, leaders can earn respect from their staff through the following actions:

Lead by example – There is nothing more powerful for employees to see than their manager working hard, smart and exuding professionalism.

Know, believe and love – Managers cannot lead unless they know, believe and love what they are doing. Employees see right through a manager who is going through the motions at work.

Care – Great leaders genuinely care about their employees and their families.

Coach – Leaders hire top performers, then let them do their job and stay out of their way. When needed these managers are there to coach, teach and support employees to help them succeed at their jobs.

In business, a person's title does not make them a great boss or leader. In fact, bad managers utilize the 'power' that comes along with their title to attempt to get things done. They are very authoritarian and unfortunately treat employees like children instead of adults.

True business leadership occurs when power and title have little to no impact on employees performing at high levels. Employees who report to great leaders are motivated to consistently seek ways to meet and exceed what is expected of them on the job. In order for this magic to occur, leaders will tell you that the formula for success to engage and motivate employees is pretty simple. It's all in what they do and what they say.

Great leaders naturally inspire employees. They also help make work more enjoyable, challenging and engaging for their staff. Their impact on morale and the overall work environment cannot be overstated. As organizations are always on the lookout for qualified employees, remember that top performers love to work for individuals who lead versus manage and actually do what they say.

64

HOW TO MAKE A POSITIVE
IMPRESSION IN BUSINESS

———————

Someone recently asked me how my former company, ERC had become so successful over the years. I shared that we had a great team and a full spectrum of relevant services. In addition, we followed some key guidelines on how we would communicate and work with each other, customers and prospective clients. These guidelines served us well and were always appreciated by those we interacted with inside and outside of the company.

Our approach to some fundamental business practices required hard work, attention to detail and an emphasis on being well-organized. In an era where electronic communications are overused and erode the human touch in business, the following rules of the road allowed our organization to stand out amongst competitors locally and nationally:

Follow up – Whether it is reaching out to a client on a big proposal or coordinating a meeting, follow up is critical to your business success. Besides being courteous and professional, timely follow up sends a positive message to clients and prospects that you are interested in working with their company.

Response time – Respond to people faster than what they expect. It is a competitive advantage and will allow your company to be seen as a business that responds and reacts quickly to change, requests and confirmations.

Return calls – Return calls and return them promptly. The same goes for electronic communications.

Pay bills on time – I have never understood why some companies feel that it is acceptable to delay payments due so they can improve their organization's cash flow. It is a terrible way to treat companies that are owed money for services rendered and/or products delivered. Everyone wants to be paid on time, so make sure that your company's bills are paid promptly.

Use the phone – Electronic communication is certainly easy and convenient but falls short when the communication dictates a more personal approach. There is nothing worse than responding to an unhappy customer with an email or text. It is amazing how easily issues resolve when you pick up the phone, call your customer and listen.

Hand-written notes – A simple follow up hand-written note makes a tremendous impression. A text with a smiley emoji pales in comparison to receiving a meaningful note in the regular mail. Sure, it is not as fast as a text or email, but the impact that is made is priceless.

Great customer service – Providing over-the-top customer service is a great business strength. Positive reputations are built on consistently over-delivering, on time and within budget. To build a legion of loyal 'raving fans', never take your clientele for granted. Be grateful for their business and always express your appreciation for clients choosing to use your organization's services.

The basic fundamentals of communicating and working with others are critically important. Whether it is paying bills on time or effectively communicating with others, in the long run your business will benefit from time-tested approaches that significantly improve the probability of success.

65

HOMEWORK FOR EMPLOYERS

Every Fall can be a significant transition for parents with school-aged children, regardless if their kids are starting kindergarten or college. And, for parents working outside the home, the transition can be even more impactful. When school starts, parents of K through grade 12 students ready themselves for major changes at home, particularly with schedules.

In addition to bus and transportation schedules, there are a number of other items that get thrown into the mix depending upon a student's participation in extra-curricular school activities. And, depending on the weather and health of the student, each day can bring its own adventure. It can get pretty crazy now and then juggling schedules and still maintaining a focus at work.

Schedule changes are not the only stressors for parents. School safety, grades, health, and social media can also add challenges for parents. And don't forget work related stress. While parents' lives change significantly during the school year, workplace schedules often do not change to accommodate school year schedules.

So if you are an employer, consider some of the following to support your employees who have school-age children:

Meetings – consider starting morning meetings at 9 am. This provides parents plenty of time to ensure that their children get off to school or day-care on time.

Family first – ensure that your employees are free to attend any school event that may fall during normal work hours. Employees can always make up time at work but can seldom make up the moments they have with their kids.

Be empathetic – having kids at school and working can be challenging at times. Stuff happens throughout the school year that can affect employees' stress levels. Whether it is grades, health, or bullying concerns, employers should recognize that some parents may come to work from time to time stressed and/ or tired due to school related issues occurring with their children. Give them a break. It is not easy these days for parents raising kids and making the effort to support a successful school experience. Also, consider the single parent household whose number of challenges are often multiplied juggling work, family and school.

Create a guilt-free environment – creating a workplace environment where parents can adjust their schedules to support the balance between work and family obligations is a great first step. For the flexible schedule program to be effective though, parents must feel that they can utilize the flex program without guilt or ramifications at work. This type of culture begins at the top. It is essential that organizational leadership embraces the importance of work-life balance, especially during the school year.

Ask – if you are wondering how to start a program or enhance a flexible schedule program already in existence, ask your employees their opinions. They will provide you valuable insight. Remember, your own employees are the best consultants to your organization.

Make it a strategy – flexible schedule programs are no longer just a nice perquisite to have in your organization. Flex programs are a key strategic initiative that support a well-structured recruitment, selection and retention program.

Manage expectations – communication of a flexible schedule program is essential. Communicate so that employees understand how to use it and that it is supported from the CEO and the rest of the organizational leadership.

Be flexible with flex – organizations that have implemented successful flexible schedule programs have discovered that a one-size fits all approach seldom works. It is important to recognize that not all employees have the same scheduling needs. Customizing a program to meet individual needs often proves to benefit the organization and employee.

Change your perspective – if you need added incentive to recognize the true value of supporting parents' crazy schedules, remember that the greatest community service any parent can provide is raising good kids. So, think of your organization making a positive impact in the community by supporting parents with school-age kids.

In this era where organizations are desperately seeking top talent to join and stay at their workplace, it is imperative to ensure that a sound flexible schedule program is in place. If your organization lacks a well-structured approach to supporting work-life balance and flexible schedules, your team might have some homework to do. On the other hand, if your flex program is up and running and working well, you deserve an A+!

66

HOW GLOSSOPHOBIA CAN HURT
YOUR CAREER

About fifteen years ago I attended a business awards dinner where one of the presenters almost fell off the stage due to an extreme case of stage fright. It was a sight I will never forget. The presenter was providing a few moments of commentary about one of the event honorees. This individual was so nervous to speak at the podium that he began shaking uncontrollably with sweat trickling down his forehead. His knees buckled and he began to fall backwards. Fortunately, he was able to steady himself just prior to falling off the back of the stage. At first the audience of nearly 1,000 thought that the presenter may have encountered a serious health issue. Their concerns were quickly alleviated when the presenter went back to the podium and announced to the gathering that he hated to speak in public and that he was just very nervous. Suffice it to say that he had not accomplished the positive impression he was hoping he might convey about himself and his firm by presenting at the event. Sadly, his worst fears of speaking in front of a large audience became reality.

The fear of public speaking, also known as Glossophobia, affects many individuals. If you have Glossophobia, and are in a job that requires public presentations, consider the following ideas to reduce your stress while improving your delivery of your presentation:

Practice, practice, practice – There is no substitute for practice. Presenting your topic aloud to yourself, friends and or family may make a world of difference when you ultimately arrive on stage. Make sure your presentation is timed and be open to feedback from those listening. You will find that these simulations allow you time to continuously refine your delivery and content.

Be ready for a disaster – Prepare as if everything will go wrong around you during your presentation such as a power outage. When you prepare for the worst you will be able to still be successful in spite of misfortune.

Know your stuff – You must know your material. Mastery of a subject allows you to speak with confidence and handle tough questions.

Know your audience – Understanding your audience's demographics, knowledge of the subject, their attention span and level of interest will aid in developing your content and delivery style.

Time of day matters – Speaking at a morning breakfast briefing is quite different than an after-dinner event. Tailor your presentation to ensure that it works for the morning, afternoon or evening audience.

Pace yourself – When you talk to fast you will lose the audience fast. A well-paced presentation allows for impactful voice inflections, pauses and the ability for the audience to follow along so they can listen effectively.

Eye contact – Engage your audience with good eye contact. Reading your presentation and/or the bullets on a PowerPoint presentation will totally turn off an audience.

Arrive early – Always arrive at least forty-five minutes to an hour early if possible. This will provide you the opportunity to scope out the physical layout, meet with event organizers and also members of the audience. This is a great way to increase your comfort level and calm your nerves prior to your presentation.

Avoid technology – The best way to avoid technology snafus during your presentation is to avoid technology. I have seen too many situations where technology failed during a speaker's talk and watched the speaker become totally lost as he/she no longer had their technology crutch to carry the presentation. If you must use some sort of technology to enhance your presentation, be prepared to effectively present the remaining portion of your talk without interruption, if technology fails you.

Finish on time – Be considerate of your audience and event planners by always finishing on time. If you have practiced your talk, then your timeliness on your presentation will be guaranteed.

Use humor and stories – Great speakers know how to use well-placed, tasteful humor and also stories that enhance their message. By using humor and stories, your presentation will be more interesting and relatable to your audience.

There may not be a total cure for Glossophobia, but using some of these ideas may increase the probability that you will be more comfortable with speaking in public. If that occurs, that will certainly be something to talk about!

67

THE PRESCRIPTION FOR GREAT CUSTOMER SERVICE

Many years ago I was the Director of Human Resources for a large group medical practice based in Northeast Ohio. This healthcare practice boasted over 100 physicians and 1,000 employees that included medical professionals and support staff that were second to none. During my nearly eight years there, I was part of an organization that grew substantially. Despite our rapid growth, we sustained a great family oriented workplace culture that made it a pleasure to go to work each day.

Though it has been a long time since I worked there, the customer service lessons learned from that experience benefited me throughout my career. Like other healthcare institutions, our patients were nervous, anxious and possibly in pain. Imagine the challenges of having customers that were in a poor mood even before they walked through your doors! That presented some unique challenges for our team and I remember us working relentlessly to figure out new and better ways to enhance their interactions with our staff.

Here are the key customer service takeaways from my days at that group medical practice that still apply today to any business:

Minimize wait times – Our physician reception areas were referred to as Waiting Rooms. Appropriately named, our Waiting Rooms were a poor start to our patients' experience due to the excessive time patients sat to see their doctor. We made significant progress to remedy that situation, yet it continued to be a work in progress. In this era of instant gratification and the need for speed, it is essential that your business minimize customer wait times on the phone, in-person or to receive your company's services and products.

Follow up – Whether it was lab or test results, many of our patients relied on physicians or their offices following up with them in a timely manner. Follow up remains important today and it is so much easier to accomplish with all of the touch points afforded through technology. What we also learned was that there was absolutely no good reason for poor follow up. Customers do not want to hear excuses for poor follow up, they would just appreciate an apology and the job done right next time.

Smile – A warm customer greeting with a smile and good eye contact is always appreciated. It makes a huge difference when customers experience a pleasant greeting on the phone or in person.

Listen and be genuinely empathetic – We knew that patients wanted their doctors and medical staff to listen empathetically to their medical concerns. Not surprisingly, the doctors with good bedside manner were typically our most highly rated physicians by our patients. Likewise, successful businesses, not only care about their customers, they listen intently to their needs and concerns with great interest.

This is all pretty basic stuff, but it can be helpful in assisting your company differentiate itself in a competitive marketplace. News travels fast these days and positive word of mouth about your customer service is the best form of advertising you can never buy.

68

A PITCH FOR BETTER SELLING

Many years ago, I placed a call to a local big box electronics store to inquire about their appliance advertisement that had caught my attention. I called the store to ask some questions about the refrigerator model that appeared in the ad.

It was mid-morning and the store, according to their ad, had been open for about an hour. Whoever answered the phone sounded disinterested and in a hurry. I asked if I could talk with a sales representative about the ad and specifically about the refrigerator that I had interest in purchasing. She replied that all the sales people were unavailable because they were all in a sales meeting. "So, if I am understanding you correctly, the sales people are in a sales meeting trying to figure out how to get people like me to come in so that they can make a sale," I commented. The receptionist did not see any humor in my response and repeated that they were all unavailable to talk with me. We concluded the call on a pleasant note and I proceeded to purchase the same refrigerator at one of their competitors who gladly price-matched the advertised offer. Incidentally that big box chain is no longer in business.

The lesson learned with this experience is that accessibility is critical as a part of the sales process. Especially in today's fast-paced business environment, if sales representatives are unavailable for prospective customers, the probability of a sale is extremely low.

In addition to accessibility, there are a host of other elements that contribute to an individual or company making a purchase decision. Here are a few in no particular order:

Response time – whether it is a business proposal or simply a telephone call to return, respond promptly to your prospective customers or be prepared to lose the sale. A quick response sends a great signal to your prospective customers that you are genuinely interested in earning their business.

No emails or texts – there is nothing I do faster online than delete random emails or texts from a salesperson asking for my business. It's like the time a text came up on my laptop from a person I had never met, from the phone store where I purchased my iPhone. The individual's text asked if I was ready to upgrade my phone. What a difference it would have made if the individual would have just called me as they already had my mobile number. Even if I would not have upgraded the phone, I would more than likely call that salesperson when I was ready to upgrade the device.

Do your research – a few years back, a software company was seeking to do business with my former company. We scheduled an introductory meeting at our offices. One individual from their organization showed up, and after exchanging pleasantries, the salesperson asked me to describe our company. Before I responded I asked the individual if he had visited our website prior to our meeting. He stated that he had not, and much to his surprise I ended the meeting. He asked me why the meeting was over, and I expressed my disappointment that he had not come prepared. When meeting a prospective customer, especially for the first time, do your research on their company and who you are going to meet. The few minutes you take to know your audience prior to meeting them will be time well-invested.

Believe in your product or service – to be truly successful in sales, you should genuinely have a passion about your product or service.

Product knowledge – in addition to knowing your audience, you need to know your product and services. Be prepared to discuss your competitive advantage and how it will contribute to your prospective customers' success. Also, I often ask a salesperson if they or their company use what he or she is selling. First-hand knowledge about the product or service is impressive and can go a long way to making a sale.

Listen, listen, listen – always listen to what the prospective customer has to say. Even if you are really great at delivering a sales presentation, you are much better off saying less and listening more.

Follow up – when is the last time a salesperson followed up with you relative to your satisfaction with what you or your company purchased? Typically, if you purchase anything these days, you are handed over to the service team or in some cases a 1-800 number! If you sell for a living, consider incorporating 6-month follow-ups to the people that have become customers due to your efforts. Check in to see how they are doing and if they are satisfied with what you sold to them or their company. These timely follow-ups will also most likely increase the probability of repeat sales with your current customers.

Sell value – I never had any interest in my former company doing business with customers that prioritized price over value. Competing on price alone is a dangerous path to go down for any business as those customers are loyal to price and not with your company's products or services.

Business development remains the lifeblood of any organization. Selling is a tough and competitive profession. Tremendous success can be realized utilizing some very simple and time-tested approaches. The only thing holding back some people from realizing sales success is them buying into actions that make a difference.

69

MY TOP 21 BUSINESS
OBSERVATIONS

One of the fun aspects of working with companies over my career was experiencing and witnessing human and organizational behavior. Like many people, I learned an awful lot from my family, work, bosses, peers, and especially those individuals who reported to me. Also, I learned more from my mistakes than from successes. So, here are my top 21 observations, not in any particular order, about work and organizations:

1. Some people want to get paid for performance until they start getting paid for performance.
2. Trust is essential if you plan to develop and maintain a great workplace.
3. If you want to know about a product, ask the service person – not the sales person.
4. Read the same books as your boss.

5. The job market is always good if you know exactly what you want, conduct a focused well-organized job search and out-hustle your competition.
6. Negotiating salary never results in a win/win scenario.
7. A shortage of skilled labor is good for business – it builds organizational character and stimulates creativity.
8. It is much better to have people quit and leave than quit and stay.
9. Many people do not handle success well, and some people have a hard time handling other peoples' success.
10. Profit is not always a good thing – it tends to mask organizational blemishes.
11. "You can't do that" are the best words to motivate entrepreneurs.
12. Consultants are not any smarter if they travel from out-of-town. When you buy products and services out-of-town you hurt local jobs.
13. Ask 50 people in your organization to describe your business and you may get 50 different responses.
14. Lawyers always win.
15. Greed and fear undermine everything at a company.
16. If you want good ideas, ask your employees first.
17. Many managers hate giving performance reviews.
18. The golden rule still works.
19. Those who "go through the motions", go nowhere.
20. Great leaders, always lead by example.
21. If you know, believe and love what you are doing you increase your odds of becoming very successful.

Over the past two to three decades, our country and the world have been through some pretty challenging times including 9/11, the Great Recession and the Pandemic. Which brings me to my "bonus" observation – that most people are incredibly resilient and somehow, some way emerge from challenging times with a renewed sense of purpose, enthusiasm and strength.

Perhaps a few of my observations hit home for you. My guess is that you have your own list of workplace and people observations, which will continue to grow throughout your career. So go ahead and have some fun and list out your top ten observations about business. Better yet, at your next staff or management retreat ask everyone to list out their top ten. The results of the exercise might be eye opening and will tell you a heck of a lot about the people you work with each and every day.

70

QUESTIONS YOU SHOULD ASK
IN AN INTERVIEW

_____

Historically, when individuals prepare for job interviews they may anticipate questions that may be asked of them to assess qualifications, skills and experience. For instance, some of the questions that might be asked include:

- What are your greatest strengths and weaknesses?

- Describe how you handled conflict in your previous position?

- Why are you seeking new employment?

- Where do you see yourself in five years?

- Why do you want to work for our company?

- How would your former boss and co-workers describe your quality of work and work habits?

- Tell me about yourself.

- What was your greatest accomplishment in your last position?

There are dozens more traditional and non-traditional interview questions. But what about questions you should consider asking the interviewer? Too often, candidates are so focused on preparing their answers for possible questions asked in an interview that they spend little time on questions they should be asking to get a better understanding of the open position, company culture and workplace practices.

If you have an upcoming interview or just want to keep these for future reference, here are some questions you may want to consider asking an interviewer during the interview and selection process (these are not in any order of importance):

- Why is this position open?
- Can you describe the company's culture?
- How will my performance be assessed?
- What will I need to do over the next year to earn the top performance rating?
- May I see a copy of your performance review form?
- Who will I report to in the organization?
- May I have a copy of the job description for this open position?
- Is the company involved in any community service projects or initiatives?
- What do employees like most about working in the organization?
- What do you like most about working at this company?

- What are the biggest challenges of this job?

- What is the most important thing I should accomplish in the first 90 days on the job?

- How will I be trained for this position?

- Beyond my initial training and orientation, will other professional development opportunities be available?

- How would you describe the company's values?

- Are the financial results of the company shared with employees on a regular basis?

- Is there anything I need to clarify about my qualifications for this job?

- When will I expect to hear from you regarding the next step in the selection process?

This list only represents a sampling of the types of questions you may want to ask an interviewer. The bottom line is that there is information you should be seeking about the job and the company if you interview for an opening. Make sure you write down and hold onto the interviewer's responses. Should you be selected as the candidate receiving an employment offer, you will want to refer back to the answers received to make a good decision about whether to proceed with employment with that company.

They say employment at a company is like a marriage. If that is so, don't go into a new job without understanding who you are about to "marry."

71

HOW DOES YOUR COMPANY REACT TO MISTAKES?

The true test of a company's character is when the chips are down. It's easy to manage and lead a company during a record year of growth and profitability. Challenging times show us which companies are innovative, creative, agile and customer focused. Leaders in organizations either rise to the occasion or miserably flop. And make no mistake, employees and customers take notice.

Tough times really test organizational infrastructure, systems, workplace policies, communications and the quality of products and services. Again, some companies flourish while others scramble for answers.

During times of business upheaval and disruption, it is not uncommon for mistakes to occur at every organizational level. Some are minor and barely noticed, while others reflect gross miscalculations. These errors are to be expected in periods earmarked by dramatic change and conditions that seemingly change daily.

How does your company handles mistakes and errors that affect the business, employees and customers? Here are a few ideas you may want to reflect on as to how your company stacks up, in the eyes of its workforce, customers and prospective customers when mistakes are made:

Nobody's perfect – A great first step is to appreciate and accept that no one is perfect at your company. This acknowledgement needs to start at the top.

Reaction – When a situation arises where an error has occurred, is the first reaction defensive? Does your corporate culture acknowledge that errors will and do occur, and that ownership of the mistake is the desired and supported behavior?

Acknowledgement – Does your company acknowledge to its customers when a mistake is truly the organization's fault? Taking "credit" for the error is the first critical step necessary to re-establishing credibility with customers.

Listen – Genuinely listen to customers' concerns and complaints. Being defensive or providing excuses does not help the problem. Simply listen to the customer, acknowledge the mistake and ask "How can we fix this issue for you?"

Timely response – The speed upon which a company responds to customer concerns can have a dramatic impact on resolving the matter. Delays in response time send a clear message to customers that your company simply does not care and can increase customer frustration with doing business with your organization.

How you respond – A friend of mine mentioned that she received an email apology from a service firm she utilizes for her company. The apology was half-hearted addressing an extremely serious error that occurred in the delivery of the firm's services to my friend's organization. As a result, my friend sought other providers for the services needed and she no longer wished to work with a firm that could not even pick up the phone to call her to address the issue. The moral of the story is to always pick up the phone when acknowledging a mistake with a customer. Electronic apologies are a great way to lose a good customer.

Mistakes are opportunities – Recognize that any mistake or error with a customer may be an opportunity to turn a bad situation into a great one. Don't just resolve the issue. Figure out creative ways to WOW your costumer with your response. It may be a big discount on their next order, eliminating the fees on the current order or some other idea that will send a message to the customer that you are sorry for the issue and are interested in keeping them as a happy client of your business.

Who is in Customer Service – Ensure that your company has the right people in place addressing customer concerns when issues arise. Aside from employees formally in customer service roles, ideally every employee in your company should be an ambassador of your business and have the ability to listen and respond well, when confronted by a customer with a service and/ or product issue.

The bottom line is to address customer issues the right way. Otherwise mistakes can turn an otherwise manageable situation and opportunity into an organizational mess that may not be recoverable.

Look, it's fun and a lot easier to run a business when everything is going your way. Yet, an organization's true reputation, future sales, customer relations, character and culture are really defined by the actions it takes when challenging issues, mistakes or errors arise.

72

THE ART OF THE THANK YOU

Towards the end of 2018, the year I left ERC, I was in the process of meeting with business partners and clients to express my appreciation for their support over the 20 years I was honored to have led the organization. The conversations held were all bittersweet. I was excited about embarking on the next chapter in my life but at the same time had a pit in my stomach as I was saying goodbye to so many tremendous people.

There was one meeting that stood out from the rest. It was with the CEO of a rather large privately held and very successful Northeast Ohio company. His organization had been a client of ours and requested project work from us on occasion. They were by no means our largest customer, but when they had a need, they would call us first. Towards the end of our conversation he asked, "Pat, do you have any idea why we kept calling your folks whenever we needed advice or had a project need?" Without waiting for my reply, he stated "Because you always gave me a call and said thank you for the work. It did not matter whether we gave you a small or large project, I always got a call from you. You need to know how much that meant to me." His statement floored me as my calls to clients were just a natural part of how we conducted business. We truly did appreciate our clients' business and did not hesitate to express our thanks. Maybe that is just another reason why ERC celebrated 100 years in business in 2020.

The Pandemic disrupted normal patterns of how and where we work. It may also have impacted relationships with clients as dependence on technology to communicate certainly dominated, due to the need to physically distance. One thing that did not change was the importance of acknowledging, appreciating and praising others. What also did not change are the many ways a thank you can be expressed, some carrying more value than others.

These days, an email, text, emoji or "Like" may not be doing the trick of expressing a genuine thank you. It may be time to get back to some of the following basics, to restore the personal approach to show your appreciation and gratitude. Here are a few ideas to consider:

Make A Call – It may be time to pick up the phone and make a call even if it is virtual. Hearing your voice and the true sentiment of the thank you goes a long way.

Handwritten Notes – If you really want to make a lasting impression, consider a hand-written thank you note. It is significantly more meaningful than an email or text and sends a message that you took time out of your day to say thanks. Sure, it is a lot slower than an electronic communication, but its impact is priceless.

Surprise Them – Catch people off guard with your gestures of appreciation. For instance, providing more time off for employees, when it's not expected is a guaranteed way to express a meaningful thank you.

Say It and Mean It – Verbalize your thank you often and with meaning. Those two words truly resonate with your employees and customers.

Make an Investment – A great way to show appreciation for your employees is to make a continued investment in their career. This can be done through ongoing conversations about their job and career path. In addition, encouraging them to participate in job-related training or seminars reinforces your interest in their short and long-term success.

Listen – Get to know what is important to your clients and employees. This is accomplished through active listening. Your time and interest will get noticed and interpreted as a positive approach to you genuinely caring.

Actions Speak Louder Than Words – How you treat people, whether they are employees, customers, past customers or prospective clients affects your credibility. Treating people well and with respect may be the ultimate way of showcasing your gratitude.

Performance Reviews – The formal performance review process is an excellent opportunity to provide constructive feedback and to say thank you for a job well done.

Timing – The quote "Timing is Everything" rings true when it comes to expressing your appreciation. Procrastination on delivering a well-deserved thank you, dilutes the message and can create a poor impression. Be timely in your feedback and that expression of appreciation will be well-received.

Consider committing to assessing the way you and your

organization say thank you. It may be a very worthwhile initiative, that if accomplished can actually change lives in a world that so sorely needs a positive lift.

73

GETTING YOUR COMPANY'S MESSAGE ACROSS

Have you ever played the Telephone Game? It is a common exercise utilized by some corporate trainers and consultants as an icebreaker to demonstrate the importance of active listening. If you are unfamiliar with the game, here is how it works:

Employees arrange themselves in a circle or a straight line. The game begins with someone whispering a phrase into the ear of the person to their right. This continues as the whispered phrase works through the players until it reaches the last person in the circle or line. The last player then says the phrase out loud, to the entire group. During the game, the phrase can only be whispered once, so each person must pay close attention. Not surprisingly, the last player typically shares a phrase that is significantly changed compared to the original phrase. The exercise is fun and provides participants a quick lesson on how easily information can be miscommunicated and misinterpreted.

Interestingly, a real Telephone Game gets played out daily at the workplace. Every day, tons of information is communicated within organizations. Information is shared across, up and down organizations with the assumption that messages are clear, concise and understood. Unfortunately, that is not always the case. In addition, even if the original communications are "clear as a bell," there are no guarantees that information will be shared and disseminated in a way that the original message stayed intact.

If you are finding that your organization's communications are poorly communicated consider these ideas:

Choose your words wisely – Ensure that your words are clear, simple and understandable.

Answer the five W's – Your communications should always address the 'who, what, when, where and why.' Oh, and don't forget to address the 'how'.

Over communicate – Most corporate messaging benefits from repetition.

Choose the right communication tools – Consider the audience when disseminating information within your organization. This will often dictate which tools will be most effective. Don't shy away from using multiple media channels to communicate information.

It starts at the top – If you are an organizational leader, have you created an environment of trust and respect in your workplace? If you genuinely listen to employees you will soon see people opening up to you like never before. You will be leading by example, and your management team will follow suit.

Staff Meetings – Encourage people to speak up at staff meetings.

If they do, don't blow their ideas out of the water. If you do squash ideas, there is little likelihood those employees will ever offer up suggestions or feedback again.

Eliminate anonymity – If you need to have employees provide feedback anonymously then you probably have a heck of a lot of work to do relative to opening up communication lines and reducing the "fear factor." Whether it is a suggestion box or an employee engagement survey, your goal should be to have employees participate enthusiastically without the need for confidentiality.

Performance Reviews – Companies that have an environment of open communications provide ongoing feedback to employees, throughout the year, rather than waiting for the traditional once a year formal performance review.

Give credit where credit is due – Ensure that you are publicly praising and rewarding employees who provide great ideas that benefit the company. It sends a wonderful, powerful and positive message to the staff that ideas are welcome and encouraged.

It starts with interviews – Make sure that candidates for open positions understand that employees are encouraged and expected to be active participants in the success of the organization.

Hire and keep the right people – Work hard at identifying the very best people for open positions and focusing on retaining the employees that drive 100% of your organization's results. Keeping employees with poor attitudes about themselves and their work will hold you back, negatively affect open communications and discourage the type of positive workplace you seek.

Hopefully some of these ideas will be helpful to you and your team. Whether it is communicating tasks, objectives, goals, news, policies, procedures or your company's missions and values, it is vital that your team attempt to minimize the distortion that naturally occurs when employees communicate with one another.

There are many more ways to support open communications with your entire staff. It takes a lot of work and happens over time. In an era where so many people hide behind electronic communications and social media to communicate, it can be challenging to maintain a high level of interpersonal communications at your organization. Yet, if you are successful, you will find that you will no longer have to ask employees their ideas anonymously and not wonder what your people are thinking.

Incidentally, it might be humorous to hear the results of a distorted message in a Telephone Game simulation, but hurting your business because of poor internal communications is not a laughing matter.

74

BUSINESS AND LIFE LESSONS FROM A "22-YEAR-OLD"

Can you imagine only having a birthday once every four years? Well, if you were born on February 29th, you know that birthdays are really special because of leap years. I knew a guy who had a leap-year birthday and ended up celebrating only 22 actual birthdays. He passed away in 2009 and unfortunately did not make it to his 90th birthday celebration. Ironically, this 89-year-old acted and had the spirit of a 22-year-old. That's probably why he lived so long.

He was orphaned by age six and was considered a self-made man. Serving in World War II, he was proud to be part of what some call the Greatest Generation. He came home after the war and met his sweetheart. Their romance lasted through 62 years of marriage and three children. He was a well-known banker for 40 years, was active in the community and eventually retired on his own terms.

His life was full by most standards, and he had few regrets. The success he enjoyed at work and with family was supported by the following core beliefs and guiding principles including:

- Have passion.
- Make family No. 1.
- Pay in cash and balance your checkbook each month.
- Support your kids' activities, but don't push them into anything.
- Don't give instruction to kids at Little League games unless you're the coach.
- Impatience is the virtue of the highly intelligent.
- Create your own luck. Work hard. Play hard. Laugh hard.
- It's OK to kiss your kids after age ten.
- It's OK to hold hands with your spouse after age 50.
- Peanut butter and jelly sandwiches are the best.
- Make sure you have replacement insurance for your house.
- Take an active interest in your grandchildren. Get down on the floor to play with them.
- Take a family portrait once in a while.
- Let the neighborhood kids play in your yard.
- Be a good neighbor. Don't gossip.

- It's OK to show your emotion. People don't know who you are without it.

- Believe in something.

- Work toward the perfect day.

He also had the following strong beliefs about business:

- Be honest with yourself and others. Those who cheat in golf or on their spouse will cheat in business.

- Stay loyal to people and companies that provide you good service.

- Keep your shoes shined and your wardrobe up to date.

- People want to get paid for performance — that's until they start getting paid for performance.

- Don't employ anyone in your company whom you wouldn't trust with your kids.

- If you want to know about a product ask the service person, not the salesperson.

- Read the same books as your boss.

- If you want to learn about an organization, spend an hour in their reception area.

- Make friends with the housekeeping staff.

- A shortage of skilled labor is good for business. It builds organizational character and stimulates creativity.

- It is much better to have people quit and leave than quit and stay.

- Always surround yourself with winners.

When you live to almost 90 years, you accumulate plenty of knowledge and wisdom. His thoughts and beliefs evolved from a combination of experience, hard work and plenty of mistakes. These are meaningful lessons from a guy who made an impact at work, in his community and at home.

Thanks, Dad.

75

THE POST-PANDEMIC
WORKPLACE

———

Covid-19 dramatically changed the way we work, perhaps indefinitely. Many changes prior to the Pandemic, like automation, approaches to staffing and workplace policies were already in progress but were significantly accelerated seemingly overnight. Virtually every facet of how we work is different now and has forced every company to materially modify operations, marketing, sales, production, communications, strategy, human resources, offices and facilities.

No one knows when the Pandemic's effect on our daily work lives will end. Whether that occurs in five months or five years, it is hard to imagine the nation's workplaces reverting back to pre-Pandemic status. Companies have spent an incredible amount of money on changing the way their businesses operate and it is unlikely these organizations divesting enhancements that improved the bottom line while enhancing employee and customer safety.

Given the changes that have transpired and those that will occur post-Pandemic, it might be a great management exercise to walk through and identify your organization's ideas and plans of what the following areas might look like when and if the virus is contained:

Office Location – I talked with a local CEO whose employees will work at home for the foreseeable future. She was sharing with me that the lease for their facility is up for renewal in the next few years. They are seriously re-evaluating their space needs for the future, as the work-from-home option has worked so well. Their space needs appear to have dramatically changed and caused this CEO and her leadership team to consider a much smaller physical workspace in the future along with permanent work-from-home scheduling options for their employees. She is not alone as company leaders have witnessed in many cases the work-from-home option has mutually benefited employees and the company's performance.

Workplace Policies and Programs – Human Resources leaders will need to evaluate current policies and programs to understand how they might work in a post-Pandemic work world. The virus disrupted many workplace polices pertaining to absenteeism, tardiness, sick-time, safety, business travel, and dress codes. As one business leader told me, "The traditional 9 to 5 workday is extinct and so are most of the policies we had in place prior to the Pandemic. We need a whole new approach to how we work, when we work and where we work."

Communication – We all know that effective communications are essential to the success of any business. There is no substitute for in-person communications, but organizational leaders are now well aware of new and different ways to effectively communicate in a challenging era. These lessons learned may translate into a hybrid approach to meetings and communications post-Pandemic.

Staffing – In a 2018 keynote presentation at a regional business event, I shared with the audience that we were at a "tipping point" relative to office automation. I went on to state that with continued technological advances, "staffing" positions with machines versus people would continue to evolve and if given a "nudge" that tipping point might accelerate automating many jobs. History will show us one day if the Pandemic was the "nudge." How organizations staff in a post-Pandemic world will be fascinating and might have significant implications on a new set of skills, education and experience that individuals will need in the future to work alongside machines.

Performance Management – This area will be really interesting in a post-Pandemic work world, especially if work-from-home options are sustained. Performance has traditionally been determined by observation at the workplace. With work-at-home protocols, performance needs to be measured purely on results, without supervision. Now is a great time to consider new and different ways your organization will assess performance during and after the Pandemic, especially if work-at-home policies continue to be utilized. This will also include taking a hard look at existing job descriptions and job expectations.

Leadership – As we all know, the real character of a person shows up during challenging times. In many cases, real leaders rose to the occasion and probably saved their businesses. Due to the Pandemic and its effect on the workplace, leaders were forced to innovate, take risks and make decisions they never thought would occur in their careers. And, it's not over. The challenges will continue and how leaders conduct themselves in the post-Pandemic era will require skill, empathy and experience. Today's companies need to ensure they have the right leaders in place to carefully and artfully navigate the rough waters ahead.

These areas are just the tip of the iceberg. There may never be a better time to assess where your company was in January of 2020, where it is now and what it may look like in a post-Pandemic world. COVID 19 changed so much and yet, the experience presents an opportunity for all of us to re-shape, re-define and re-imagine workplaces for continued success.

www.ingramcontent.com/pod-product-compliance
Lightning Source LLC
Chambersburg PA
CBHW060231050426
42448CB00009B/1388